Eileen!

ALIVE

*A Courageous Story of Addiction,
True Love and Forgiveness*

Eileen DeClemente

ISBN 0-7414-4578-6

Published by:

PUBLISHING.COM

1094 New DeHaven Street, Suite 100
West Conshohocken, PA 19428-2713
Info@buybooksontheweb.com
www.buybooksontheweb.com
Toll-free (877) BUY BOOK
Local Phone (610) 941-9999
Fax (610) 941-9959

Printed in the United States of America

Printed on Recycled Paper

Published January 2008

Acknowledgments

I have written this book in the hope that it will help people suffering with the same disease. To all of you I wish you the best.

To my wonderful daughters Missy and Sara. I could not be more proud of the people you have blossomed into. Your hearts and souls make you loving, caring people who would never turn your backs to anyone. You both are honest and have worked hard for everything you have achieved and your achievements have been outstanding. When life has gotten sad and hard for us again, especially as we deal with my Alzheimer's, neither of you have shown anything but gratitude for what we do have—each other. None of us know how long it will be with the progression of this disease I know some weeks it has to get frustrating for you, but you always show me unending support and love. I am so fortunate to have been given the both of you as my children. I absolutely adore both of you.

To Curtis, we made it! I love you. Curtis can you believe we made it to thirty-three years and we still love each other? You are my best friend and I am so sorry I have brought this pain of fear once again into our marriage. I thought my addiction was horrible enough and now we are dealing with this Alzheimer's. I know it has changed your life, and just when we thought we were beginning the best years of our life. It still can be. I know my personality has changed but I am still in here, humor has been a big part of our relationship and it still is. I want happiness for you and 'till the day I stop knowing who you are I will do everything I can to make these days the best for us. I love you, thank you for thirty-three years of you.

To my adorable grandson Aiden. I love you and thank you so much for all you have done to make this book happen—if it was not for you this past year I could not have done it.

To my Dad, I love you and thank you for always being you. I owe my courage and strength that I eventually found in myself to you—you instilled wonderful qualities in your children and brought us up the best you could. Dad I am sorry for the pain I caused you. Thank you for your love and your patience.

To my closest sister, thank you for letting me back in your life. I missed you so much all those years.

To my Uncle Humphrey and Aunt Caroline, thank you for the short time you gave me as a child. I have never forgotten the short time you allowed us into your home— all nine of us—and you treated us with love. You made it possible for me to see what it was like to be a kid—they are my happiest childhood. I am sorry it has taken so long to tell you. I have always loved both of you.

Karen and Linda, you are special people. You gave me a special gift at a time in my life when I needed it most. I could actually go to school and not be scared all day to go home to a beating or my mother's terror. You allowed us to play and laugh and just be kids; it was so wonderful.

To the people who had so much patience with me and taught me so much when I was just learning to be a person, Gene Anne Dull, Ruth Tyndell, Jan, and everyone at the school district where I worked—those were the best years of my life. Thank you for not judging me and letting me be me.

I also dedicate this book to Penny Sansevieri of Author Marketing Experts, Inc., without her encouragement and confrontation I would have never completed this project. Finding you was the best thing that ever happened to me. You have been there every step of the way helping me write this book. You were the one to call me on my stuff when I was at my worst. You will never know how much I have grown to care and love you. Thank you so much. I will never forget you.

I want to thank my editor Jeniffer Thompson of Monkey C Media. You have made a masterpiece. I am so fortunate to have had you as an editor and your husband Chad's talents on this project. You have taken this true story and made it so others can understand the pain and healing we experienced; now others can know there is hope and help out there. You are a wonderful person and I love you.

To Jerry Simmons, thank you for your support; it has meant a great deal to me.

Thank you New Dawn for giving me my life!

CHAPTER ONE

The Fall

I could barely open my eyes. My body felt cold and numb. Where the hell was I?

What was all that noise? Fear was setting in fast as I began to shake uncontrollably. The room was a complete blur. Slowly I tried to focus on a figure of a man in the room. He had light-colored hair, but I had no idea who he was. It was then, as he slowly came into focus, that I started to cry.

He told me to stay still. He looked angry.

All at once I began to recognize my surroundings; it was my kitchen; I was on the floor. The light-haired man was wrapping something around my arm. Suddenly I could hear crying.

Oh God, what just happened?

I started to get up, but someone else who I couldn't see told me to stay down; all I wanted to know was where the crying was coming from. I recognized that cry, terror flashed through me and at once I felt vomitous—a burning feeling of fire rose up through my throat and into my mouth—someone got a pan. I didn't care. I needed to see who was crying. I started to shake as silent tears poured down my cheeks; the smell was horrific, but nothing mattered to me now—I had to know who was crying.

I struggled to look sideways, but someone's hand held my chest down. Fighting to turn my head just a little farther I caught a slight glimpse of my eight-year-old daughter Sara. A third man, whom I hadn't seen before, was kneeling next to her. I remember it like it was yesterday: She stood next to that strange man just shaking and crying. My eyes didn't leave her face, I couldn't tell you what the man looked like, I didn't care what he looked like; I felt an unbearable pain as I watched her cry. I lifted my arm to reach out for her, but the light-haired man pulled it back. I could feel the tremors take over my body as I tried desperately to reach out to her—but he won, he looked so angry as he pulled my arm back into place.

Realization hit me all at once. These men were medics; they were treating Sara for shock.

What have I done?

These poor children. What the hell kind of a mother am I?

Disgusted with myself I let out a low, guttural moan.

I can't keep doing this to my family.

My body refused to be still. The shaking was incontrollable. All I could think about was how badly I wanted to hold my baby. She was upset. She needed me. Panic began to set in and I felt hysterical, completely out of control. Wanting nothing more than to reach Sara, I looked up to see everyone in the room glaring at me. All I saw was anger—all I wanted was Sara.

Her cries melted into quiet sobs as the man told her: "Your mom is okay honey, she's going to be okay, everything is going to be okay."

Her little eyes just stared at me. Exhausted from the struggle, I let my head lay on the cold tile as these men did who-knows-what to me. I stared up at the ceiling. It was as if every bit of life was leaving my body. Then I started to remember.

***

Sara and I were home alone watching TV. She kept looking at me with this odd look.

"What's the matter?" I asked her.

"Are you okay, Mom?"

"What do you mean?"

"Well you look like...." and she stopped suddenly.

"What?" I asked.

"Nothing. You just look tired, that's all."

"I'm not tired. Do you want something to drink?" I asked.

"Okay," she said. I stood up to go into the kitchen, but I could feel her eyes following me.

"I'll help you," she said suddenly as she jumped up from the couch and started to follow me toward the kitchen. I got a little irritated, but didn't want her to notice so I just told her to sit back down.

"I'll get it," I said. As I walked into the kitchen and opened the refrigerator door, my legs started to tremble and a familiar feeling overcame me; every inch of me was shaking; I could feel myself going down—everything went black.

***

I was told that I had had a seizure. That had been the familiar feeling. It was not my first—it was one of many over recent years.

Common to a seizure, my body shook uncontrollably. Again and again my head banged against the freezer until I bit my tongue, spewing blood onto the floor around my head. Sara tried her best to piece together the events that led to my fall for the medics.

At the time, her older sister, Missy, had been spending the night with friends across the street. Sara ran out onto the porch screaming for help. We still don't know who called the ambulance, but the medics arrived soon thereafter. Missy saw the lights from across the street and ran home as fast as she could. She now tells me that she ran up to me to see if I was okay. In a daze I reached out and touched her face and said, "Oh, what a pretty little girl." She was terrified, she didn't know what was wrong with me, but she knew it was serious.

This I remember: Sara kept telling me how much she loved me. She just stared at me saying over and over: "Mom you can't die, you can't die."

As I started to say something, the man with the light hair (who I thought was angry with me) interrupted me: "Your

3

mom is not going to die, honey. We need you to calm down for your mom and go into the other room with your sister."

Missy, tears streaming down her face, was just walking into the room. She couldn't say anything, she just bent down and put her arm around the top of my head. She stayed completely still for what seemed like five minutes, but was just seconds. The man put his hand on her shoulder and started to say something—she just looked at him with anger, her bottom lip quivering. She said: "No. I want to be with my mother," and then she put her arm around Sara. Holding each other, my girls burst into tears.

"What have I done; what am I doing to my family?" I screamed.

Everyone just stared down at me. I felt like everyone was judging me. And perhaps they were judging me. I deserved to be judged. They had every right to be angry with me.

I am a terrible person, I kept saying to myself. As always, my girls were the ones who came to my rescue, "it's okay Mom," they both had said.

Just then my husband walked in. "No, it's not okay." He glared at me with a look that said *I have a lot more to say, but can't because of all these people*; he remained silent.

It was then that I knew everything was going to get a lot worse. His anger was so obvious. He couldn't hide it—things got very quiet as they prepared me for the ambulance.

"I'll take her to the hospital," my husband said.

"Mr. DeClemente, that's out of the question. Your wife is not stable; she may need medical treatment on the way to the hospital."

Reluctantly he agreed, but told them he wanted me to go to a specific hospital—not the closest one they would have normally taken me to. I knew why. He just glared at me as he leaned down and said: "You are going to see doctor R. and you are going to tell him what you have really been doing; I can only imagine what is in your system and I am done covering for you. You are on your own."

I just cried. I had not shed a real tear for years; I had not felt anything in years.

I was physically sick for what I had been doing to my girls their whole life, and yet selfishly sick because I knew for the first time my secrets were out. I had been spiraling downhill for a while, drinking and drugging to extreme excess. One of the medics looked at me and quietly said: "You have an opportunity to make a change. I hope you take advantage of it, for yourself and your family. You have two wonderful daughters and your husband will cool off." I stopped crying and looked at him, there was no anger in his face. The anger I had seen in him was the anger I had for myself.

My husband was finished with enabling me, he was mad, real mad and that was not going to go away, he was done feeling for me. I was done feeling. I had self-medicated for so long that I was incapable of feeling. Our marriage had been going up in flames for some time. There were many reasons, but mainly because of my addiction; but also because of choices he had made.

The girls started begging their dad to let them go to the hospital with him. Sara, with tears running down her face said: "If you don't let us go, I'll never speak to you again."

He snapped back and told her she was not going.

"Please let me talk to her," I cried. I asked her to please stay with the neighbors because it would be late when we came home and she and her sister would just get tired at the hospital.

Missy stomped her feet and looked at me with hatred. "Are you going to come home tonight?" she asked angrily.

I can't explain how that look and the sound of her voice made me feel. I started to cry again.

The girls had never seen my cry before. I was usually like a robot. I rarely went anywhere or did anything; I was motionless with no facial expressions, mostly I just sat and stared.

This was different, Missy was watching me cry and it was making her mad. I could see the resentment building in her; it was not what she said, but what she didn't say.

She looked at her sister and took her hand, "come on."

Sara snapped back at her: "Don't be mean to Mom, Missy, she can't help it."

Her father looked at her, "no Sara, she CAN help it and she is going to start helping herself now."

Sara just got more upset and continued to cry. The medics were trying to get me into the ambulance and interrupted my husband to tell him we were leaving. By this time, I was going numb, the end was coming, my life as I knew it was over—our secrets were out. My mind was spinning a million miles a minute and my head pounded in crashing waves of one-part realization, two-parts physical exhaustion. I kept thinking back to the past month and the hell I had put my children through—the hell my husband and I had created for our children. I had been an addict for twenty-three years, using both alcohol and drugs—this was the end, my addiction had reached its peak.

The Beginning of the End

My tolerance had gotten so high that I was up to eighty pills a day—that and the drinking—I was taking anything I could to reach that familiar state of numbness. But, the fact was, I was no longer reaching a high, I just maintained—I was barely able to get up in the mornings and function. I had so many physical problems. I had nearly died so many times that I had lost count. I was slipping away.

If it wasn't the seizures, it was my complete loss of bodily functions. I spent most of the day passed out while my body took the liberty of urinating or my bowels would empty wherever my body would land, on the couch, in the tub, the kitchen floor.... Our furniture was destroyed—I should have been humiliated, but I didn't feel anything.

My husband was so disgusted with my behavior. I could tell by the way he looked at me.

"You make me so mad, I feel sick every time I look at you," he had once said. Alcohol was one part of his coping mechanism, extramarital relationships was the other part. I had known about it for years, but getting my drugs and booze were more important. If I didn't address it, it was like it wasn't happening, and at that point—I just didn't care.

I started getting numerous phone calls from someone who would not reveal her name; she gave me specific information warning me that Curt was going to leave and take my children with him. To this day I don't know who she was, but I assume she was Curt's mistress. That wasn't important—the real issue was that my addiction was the problem, I was more scared for the girls than for myself, so I confronted him. He told me that he was in love with another woman and he wanted to be with her.

To my surprise I fell apart. I got down on my hands and knees and begged him: "Please don't leave me, I need your help. I will die if you leave and take my girls."

I remember pushing him against the wall and throwing myself at him and just begging him to help me. We both started to cry and he looked at me and said: "I don't know what I'm going to do."

All this happened in the last month before my fall; I learned later that the girls had known everything—they had also overheard our conversation. How was it that I was allowing my addictions to control me? The choices I was making were destroying my girls—and yet, I loved them more than anything. I was out of control.

If I love them so much, how can I be doing this? How can they believe anything I say?

Sadly, I had experienced a similar childhood, a childhood filled with abuse and neglect that had filled me with pain and worry. Here I was repeating the same behaviors with my own children.

I don't even remember them strapping me into the ambulance, all I could think about was the final days that had led up to that moment. My thoughts were interrupted by a kind voice: "Are you okay?" It was the light-haired man, the one I thought was mad at me.

"No, I'm not, how can I be all right?" I felt like an out-of-control bobble-head, my head moving back and forth, exasperated and scared. I cried: "I'm never going to be all right. I have ruined everyone's life."

"Poor you," a voice echoed from outside the ambulance. It was Curt. "You're right. Our lives are ruined."

"Excuse me sir, I need to close the doors. We will see you at the hospital."

"I don't know if I'll be there," he barked back at the medic.

"Well, that's up to you, we need to leave now sir." I could hear the door creak to a final slam and the engine startup with a sudden finality that I'll never forget.

"He is just angry," the voice said. "You need to focus on more important things right now, like getting yourself better."

"I don't know what better is, I don't even know what is wrong with me."

"Oh I think you do." These men were not angry with me; they were simply doing their jobs.

"I am so ashamed. You saw my daughters, they are a mess... and I did it... and I am going to lose them if I don't stop what I'm doing, my husband hates me... he is so mad... I hope he doesn't go to the hospital... I don't want him there...."

I fell into a dazed stupor. I could hear myself talking, but I didn't know what I was saying. All I could feel was something tight around my arm again.

"Mrs. DeClemente, can you hear me, can you hear me?"

I started to get irritated, "Yes I can hear you. I don't want to talk anymore. I don't want to do anything anymore."

Everything from that point was a blur until I was jarred awake by the shaking of the bed. It kept jumping all around and bumping into things, or so it felt like.

"What is going on? Where am I?"

"You're at the hospital, we are going to be here a few minutes and then we'll be leaving. Okay?"

"No! I don't want you to leave—I thought you were angry with me, but you're not, you're a very nice man."

I started feeling lightheaded and got this overwhelming need for a drink, or some drugs, anything to make me feel better. I started to shake and tremble all over.

"My head hurts," I kept saying. "My head hurts so bad."

Two nurses were rolling me into a small room with a curtain surrounding it. One of them pulled the curtain back; it was so loud it made me want to vomit again.

"Why are you making so much noise? My head hurts!"

"I'm sorry. Show me where it hurts."

I tried to lift my arm but I was shaking too much. I started to cry, "What is wrong with me? Why can't I stop shaking? I can't stop shaking. My head hurts," I was babbling incoherently. My head hurt so bad, all I could think about was where I could get my next fix. I needed something—anything.

"I am going to get sick...."

Someone ran over to me with a plastic bowl or something. I heard voices coming toward me, men's voices, but I couldn't make out what they were saying. The curtain pulled open and I saw Curt.

"I thought you weren't coming? You didn't have to come. You should have stayed with the girls...."

"Stop it Eileen; just stop!"

I felt that familiar rage building inside me.

I hate it when he tells me what to do. I hate it.

I looked up but everything was blurry. I made out the figure of another man standing there.

"Just relax Eileen. Just relax and tell me what happened tonight," it was Dr. R.

"I had a seizure."

"By the looks of you, it was a bad one. You're in rough shape."

"I have a headache."

"She has a headache because she wants drugs." My husband spoke up. I looked at him with as much anger as I could conjure up.

"Calm down Eileen. Is that true?"

I started to cry a different cry. It was a cry that I could feel deep inside me.

I needed a fix. It had been hours since I had taken anything. My previous feelings of guilt were being overshadowed by my need for drugs.

I looked up and this time I could see the doctor very clearly. Dr. R. had been on call that night and had come straight from home. His hair was long in the front and very blonde that night. He had on plain clothes—not the suit I was used to seeing. He was not happy—I could see that. I started to get that feeling of panic again. I felt cornered.

"What did you take tonight, Eileen?"

Curt was glaring at me; waiting for me to answer.

"What did you take tonight? Let's start there."

He put his hand on my arm to help stop the shaking. I couldn't look at him. I couldn't tell him. He was one of the doctors that I had been manipulating for prescriptions, but he knew that now. He knew everything before he even walked into the room, my husband had made sure of that. Even so, he wanted to hear it from me.

"Eileen it's over, I need you to tell me everything. Start at the beginning. What did you take, or drink?" His voice was calm. He was a very tall man, but he looked even taller that night.

I started sweating. Through my tears I looked up at him and said: "Pills. A lot of pills."

"Were you trying to hurt yourself?" he asked.

"No." I answered. "I needed them."

"How many pills are we talking about?"

I just kept looking at him though I could feel my husband's eyes piercing through me. Curt started to get mad. "Our daughters can't keep watching their mother do this to herself. They have seen it too many times. In fact, they don't think their mother is going to come home tonight."

"She's not," said the doctor. "Look at her."

"No, I mean they think she's going to die. They've seen her *almost* die so many times that they don't know if they're ever going to see her again. It's like this everyday for them. Every time they go to school, they never know if she'll be there at the end of the day. On the weekends they are afraid to leave her alone."

"Well I am going to be honest with you," said Dr. R., "as far as your physical health is concerned, you are dying. I'm not trying to scare you; I think you both know how serious this is. Look at yourself. Your shaking is caused by a drug-induced Parkinson's. Your liver is enlarged. Your tests reveal much more."

I just laid there lifeless; by then I didn't care. I wanted to die. I detested myself. There was nothing to like about me. I had emotionally abused my family for years—the family I loved.

"I am just like my mother, Doctor."

"You are not your mother, you are nothing like her so let's just talk about what is happening now. What did you take tonight? What do you take and drink on a daily basis?"

That question again. I couldn't say it. His facial expressions were changing and his eyes were so serious that I thought maybe he actually cared. No one said anything while I looked away sobbing.

"Pain pills, Valium, antidepressants, sleeping pills, pot, cocaine, muscle relaxers, alcohol and anything else I thought might get me high," I finally blurted out. "But, I haven't felt high or drunk in a long time. The pills don't give me the feeling they used to."

"What do you mean you don't feel the same way?"

"They used to give me a buzz, but they don't anymore. They just make me feel like I'm not going insane—and I don't feel like I am going into withdrawal."

"How do you know you're going into withdrawal?"

"I've had that feeling many times before when I start running out of pills and couldn't get any booze."

"And what happens?" He was irritated. His voice changed, it got lower and his eyes were staring right through me.

Why is this making him so mad? I thought to myself.

"I get bad stomach cramps. I sweat and shake more than usual, then it starts to feel like I'm going to panic."

"What do you mean panic? Do you mean anxious?"

"Yes, I guess so."

"Well, which is it?"

I started to cry again. I felt scared and my body felt funny; my heart started pounding faster and faster.

"What are you afraid of, Eileen?"

"Why are you getting mad?" I asked him.

Curt interrupted: "He's mad for the same reason everyone is mad."

Doctor R. looked at Curt: "Why are you mad, Curt?"

"Because I am sick of it. I am sick of the girls seeing her like this and they see her like this more than I do. They don't know exactly what is going on with her but they know it has something to do with the pills she takes and the drinking, which is all the time if she can help it."

"Is that true, Eileen?"

"Yes!" yelled Curt. His voice was escalating and he was staring at me with a look of hatred. "Why do you think the girls fight all the time? They are fighting over YOU. Missy gets angry with you and Sara gets angry with her for being mean to you."

Looking straight at him I started to scream: "I know, I KNOW, I hate myself." I was crying and trying to catch my breath. "I am so sorry. I know you don't believe me. I love my girls. I don't want to be this way. Do you hear me? I DON'T WANT TO BE THIS WAY. I don't want to get out of bed in the morning. I want to be like everyone else. I am begging you, Doctor. I need help. I don't know what to do. I'm afraid. I don't know how to live any other way."

Snot was running down my face and into my mouth, I was choking through my tears, trying to tell them how sorry I was, how bad I wanted to change, to fix me forever. I was disgusting. I was drenched in stench and sweat and puke and blood. I couldn't stand myself. I felt like a hopeless piece of crap.

"When did things get this bad, you two?" asked Doctor R.

"They've always been bad," Curt answered, "but it's gotten worse the past eight years, and even worse this last year when her mother died on Eileen's birthday. They hated each other. So, I decided we were moving and getting away from her family. They were sick of it too and I didn't want her using them as an excuse to drink and drug."

Everything got quiet for a minute, just long enough for me to get even more agitated and angry (at myself). I looked right into the doctor's eyes, "I know I'm dying. The only reason I don't want to die is because of what it will do to my girls. I urinate blood half the time; I don't get periods; I've lost my teeth—either because of malnutrition or the car accidents—or maybe the ten times I've fallen down the stairs and knocked them loose, so here I am at thirty-four with false teeth; I throw up every time I eat," I was getting louder now, nearly screaming, "I've ruined the furniture by passing out and losing control of my bowels and bladder and sometimes I am not even passed out when it happens."

Everything was so quiet, you could have heard a pin drop; it was like time had stopped for a brief moment and my heart sank into my stomach with a silent thud.

The doctor leaned against the wall for what looked like support. The nurse had tears running down her face. "Doctor," she asked, "have you ever heard of anyone taking eighty or ninety pills a day?"

He didn't answer. He was staring at the floor.

For the first time, Curt was looking at me as if he cared.

I looked at him. "When I get better, whenever that is, you can leave, Curt. I am so sorry. I am so sorry."

"Let's get you cleaned up," said Doctor R. "I need to make some phone calls and set up a plan to keep you from going into withdrawal until you can get the help you need. I'm not an expert in this area, but I am going to talk to some people who are. I'm going to be honest with you Eileen, I don't know if you will get better physically, but you can stop doing this. It will be a miracle if you do live through this. But, I've seen miracles happen, if that's what you choose to call them. If you use or get drunk one more time I believe that will be it for you. The choice is yours. Your body is maintaining. That's why you're not getting high any more. You'll probably never get that feeling again. Are you hearing me? Eileen?"

"Yes."

"You have done some permanent damage to your body and your brain Eileen."

I had my eyes and ears fixed on everything he was saying and it didn't feel fuzzy to me—that was different. By now, my husband was standing there with his hand over his face not saying a word.

Doctor R. put his arm around Curt: "Let's go out into the hall and talk a bit."

Before he walked out he put his hand on my arm. I just looked at him with tears streaming down my face; he winked and they walked out.

Shaking uncontrollably, I tried to raise my arm up over my face. I had not cried a sincere cry since I was a little girl. I hadn't let myself care about anything enough to shed a tear over, except my family; however my tears had been used to manipulate and to get them to forgive me, they had always been selfish tears. Feelings were something that I couldn't handle, so I used drugs and alcohol to self-medicate me from anything painful.

The room was empty and for a moment. I felt scared and alone, then two nurses walked in. They were both smiling, which made me wonder what they were smiling about. I hadn't smiled in years.

"We are going to get you cleaned up and comfortable. Okay?"

"Yeah, that's okay. I can't stop sweating, my stomach hurts and I think I'm going to puke."

They brought out a small tray from a drawer next to me and put it under my chin. I vomited and heaved until I thought I would puke up my innards. They put a cold cloth on my head and started cleaning me up. They started to roll me over, to change my gown when all of a sudden my legs started to shake—the shakes crawled through my limbs like a small earthquake. I couldn't control it. They called in the doctor.

He came in while Curt stayed in the hall. He took my blood pressure and gave the nurses directions. I felt numb inside and out. The shakes were coming in waves. I was used to it, at home every time I tried to go up the stairs my legs would wobble and shake so bad that I would fall sometimes nine or ten steps to the bottom. It wasn't unusual for me to be lying there when my girls came home from school. They would get hysterical.

Sometimes I would get halfway up the stairs and they would have to come and help me down, which was very scary because I would have to sit on each step for five minutes or longer before I could move again.

How disgusting to put your daughters through that, I thought and I burst out crying again.

"Try not to worry," one of the nurses said, "we'll find out what is going on."

"That's not it," I said. "I know what is going on. I am doing this to myself."

The doctor was moving me from side to side trying to sit me up, which was nearly impossible; his facial expression changed—he looked worried.

"This is serious, isn't it?" I asked.

"Let me take care of this. Right now I need to make my phone calls but the nurses will take you to your room." Before he left he turned to me, his face wasn't red anymore. Softly he said: "This is your chance. Things can't get any worse for you unless you die—you don't want that, I know you don't or you wouldn't be here now. I'm going to do my part right now. You have to do the rest. You aren't complaining now, but I know how bad you must feel. You are going into withdrawal Eileen. I'll see what I can do to keep you comfortable."

I started crying again. "Okay." I thanked him over and over again. He nodded and smiled at me. That was the second time someone had smiled at me. It felt good, but it didn't take away the guilt and remorse that I was feeling and the total disgust I had for myself.

I wouldn't wish those feelings on anyone.

The nurses were finishing up. I felt clean, but I started sweating almost instantly. The cramps in my stomach were getting worse. One of the nurses looked at me and said: "You can do this—you have to believe in yourself."

I whispered a feeble "thank you."

"We are going to take you upstairs. The doctor is on the phone now getting you some medication."

I started to think about what lay ahead of me—about going through detox; I knew this was nothing compared to what I was going to experience. I knew because I had experienced it before—it was hell. I deserved hell.

My husband walked in, his face was red. I could tell he had been crying. I was surprised. We just looked at each other—he came over and kissed me on the head, "I'll see you sometime tomorrow."

He hated hospitals. He had spent so much time in them because of me. To this day he won't go in them unless he has to; they only bring back bad memories for him. He gets very resentful. There was so much anger between us. He had been going outside the marriage, who could blame him? I was supposed to be a wife—that's how he justified his actions. Today he outwardly admits that it was wrong.

The girls didn't miss a thing. They knew everything. How awful was that? Those poor innocent children were being robbed of their childhood. I will never forgive myself for that. There are many things I will never forgive myself for.

I was alone, crying for my family, crying for all the people who were victimized by my actions, crying for myself.

No matter what happens I will always be a horrible person.

I believed that very strongly. I had only known that horrible person inside myself.

They took me to my room. I was silent. I knew that the nurses knew why I was there. That was not important to me. I was never concerned about what the outside world thought about me. I did care how the people I loved felt about me. That was all I could think about.

They put me in my own room. I had a lot of time to think that day. I was starting to remember things I didn't want to remember, like the lies and stories I had told people in my life. As a child it had started as a means of getting attention from my mother. Then I told stories to make people think my life was as good as theirs. It got out of control. I started believing my own lies. I lied when I didn't need to lie. When I was in my addiction, I lied to get what I wanted, drugs! Now I knew I had to change. *Can I even do that?* CHANGE. It scared me. What would that mean for me? I had to take responsibility for myself. I had no clue what that would be like.

Finally the nurse came in with some medication: "The doctor ordered this; it's for your symptoms and to help you sleep. You are all wet again. Here, let me change your gown."

I didn't move or speak. I was paralyzed. She changed my gown and left. I was so tired from all the emotion and crying. I could feel the medication starting to take effect, immediately I started to feel better physically. It surprised me because I knew how high my tolerance was. It had gotten to the point that I could take 30 prescription Tylenols with codeine and not get high.

That night I went to sleep. I didn't hear a thing until my eyes opened the next morning. It was very strange. At first I didn't know where I was or what had happened. I was dripping in sweat; my bed was totally drenched.

"Good morning, you slept very well." The nurse's voice jerked me into realty—and then I remembered.

"I have your medication," she said. "You're all wet. So is your bed. Let's get you changed."

Two nurses started to roll me over. It was the same thing, I started to shake again and instantly I started to cry. It scared me every time it started. I couldn't hold back the tears, they just came and wouldn't stop—I couldn't talk.

"You'll be okay Mrs. DeClemente, you're overdue a few hours with your meds, that's why you feel the way you do."

"No that's not the reason," I snapped back. I knew the reason: I felt guilt and disgust for myself; as soon as I woke up it all came rushing back. Especially those last eight years, they had been the worst. Before then my victims had been my husband, my father, and myself, but then the girls came—they were the innocent victims.

Overwhelmed and distressed with so many foreign emotions, I found myself gasping for air, my mind was going a million miles an hour; nothing made any sense. I wished I had never admitted anything, panic was setting in; I needed to get out of there.

How could this be happening? No one has done the things I have... they are going to take my children away—I know it. I can do this myself. I can stop the pills and the drinking. I would feel like hell for a while, but I could get through it—I know it. What am I going to do? Curt won't help me anymore. He's done.

A constant stream of tears soaked my clothes and face.

I have to stop. This is the only chance I have left. I have no chances left....

With difficulty I tried to turn myself over, tried to cover my face so no one could see me. All of a sudden I started thinking about a friend whose child was critically ill, and a relative I cared about, but had never shown it, and anyone else I knew who had it worse than I did, which was millions of people. I have no idea why I started to think that way, but I'm glad I did. I had wasted twenty-three years of my life being self-destructive and yet I knew people who were dealing with problems they had not brought on themselves.

Immediately I stopped crying and began to see all the good things in my life. I had not thought that way since I was a kid and yet, back then, my life seemed like it couldn't get any worse. My mother was abusing us, my dad was constantly getting fired, and we kids were being separated from each other—but my dad always talked to us about the good things in life and taught us to be grateful for what we did have. He would play this game with us where we all had to come up with good things in our life and the last and most significant thing we would always come up with was that we had each other, and that was all that mattered.

I don't even know if my father realizes what a beautiful gift he had given us by teaching us to be grateful.

Today I can tell you that the number one thing I learned after getting sober was that my addiction had left me mentally, physically, and spiritually bankrupt. I was spiritually starved and that night in the hospital was the first indication of how bad I really was.

It was that night that I realized how long it had been since I had thought of someone or something other than myself. I never did fall back to sleep that night. All night I felt a huge lump in my throat and an acid churning in my stomach. A nurse came in—it must have been obvious that I was having a hard time because she offered to talk with me.

"Call me Eileen," I said, "and yes I would like to talk. I am such a bad person. I can't believe I have finally admitted this to myself, obviously people who know me already know what kind of a person I am."

I must have looked scared to death. It felt like my eyes were bugging out of my head and that familiar feeling of fear was overtaking my body, it was crawling up my stomach, across my neck and contorting my face into a twisted mass of emotions. My skin felt like it was burning from the inside out. I wanted to run and hide, to escape the fear and the guilt—and the pain. It would have been so much easier to just end it, but the thought of my girls made me realize that the easy way out was not an option for me.

"I have to face them, I have to deal with what I have done to my daughters," as I said it out loud, the reality of what lay ahead was perhaps the scariest thing I had ever faced.

I was scared to death.

I was losing control.

"You're right, you do have to face your daughters and the things you have done. I'm sure some of those things are probably pretty bad, I can't imagine being in your place."

"You don't want to be in my place, I have a million other terrible things I've done to other people—just thinking about them is making me sick to my stomach, some of these things I should go to jail for, and by the time this starts to unfold, I just might."

Crying and sobbing, I looked up at the nurse through swollen eyes and to my surprise she wasn't shocked, she didn't seem at all disgusted with me like everyone else I had come in contact with. I had never studied people's faces as much as I had in those two days; I had never cared enough, or maybe I hadn't the guts to make eye contact for fear of what I would see. In this gentle woman, I didn't find what I was looking for—disgust.

"How am I going to deal with all the terrible things I have done?" My throat felt stuffed with giant cotton balls, I had sores on the corners of my mouth that stung when I spoke and were getting worse with each new word; every time I thought of dealing with what I had done, the muscles in my stomach began to clench and squeeze like a vice inside of me; my heart was beating so fast that I was certain I was having a heart attack.

"I don't know how you will deal with it, but you have to be strong. Some of the consequences may seem like too much at times, but try to remember what your girls and your husband have endured because of your addiction."

I just stared at her. Normally I would have gotten defensive and have gone into a rage, blaming everything I had done on the bad things that had happened to me. But, she had just said the most important thing I would hear throughout the whole journey.

I don't know what the doctor meant when he talked about me having a disease and alcoholism being inherited, but I knew I had a lot to learn. There was a whole lot I didn't know because I had taken myself out of life and most of living is learning. I had stopped learning. I had stopped growing.

Since the first time I had taken a drink at eleven years old, I had become an alcoholic—it was then that I stopped growing, both spiritually and physically. My drinking had stunted my physical growth and had left me spiritually and socially void.

I was still staring at the nurse; I couldn't believe what she had said and how much it had affected me. She was right.

"You should try to get some sleep, you have a lot ahead of you."

I couldn't stop thinking and predicting what was going to happen. I felt like I had lost total control of my life and what was going to happen, but looking back, I know I never had it.

When I opened my eyes, the doctor was standing over me.

"We need to talk," he had said.

"What's the matter?"

"I spoke to the people at the treatment center and they will be expecting your call tomorrow." His face was very serious and stern; his eyes were wide-open and staring right at me. I looked him in the eyes.

"Do you remember everything that I explained to you last night? Or is all that fuzzy?"

"No, surprisingly it's not. Nothing is fuzzy since the seizure; I'm not used to this. Everything is usually a total blackout or things are just a blur. Something is different this time and I am not just saying that to manipulate you, something is different with me. I don't want to die, Doctor. I don't want to lose my family. I'll do anything, no matter what it takes to change."

He just looked at me for a moment, "you know, Eileen, I almost believe you. I want to believe that you mean this. Looking at you right now, I can see that there is something different in your face, something I haven't seen before."

"I'm not going to do the same thing I have done every other time when I would get home from the hospital after scaring everyone to death and then usually talking so fast that no one else could get a word in edgewise. I promise. I promise it's never going to happen again. I am going to change; I'm not going to get my girls' hopes up and then let everything go back to the way it used to be. I'm just like my own mother." A lump came from nowhere and got stuck in my throat.

He interrupted, "then why are you doing this to those girls? You know just how they feel, don't you?"

"Yes," I answered meekly.

"You'll have to excuse me," he said, "I don't know enough about this disease to understand why or how you could do this, but, I do know that it's the addiction. I'm going to leave now; I'm leaving your prescriptions with the nurses. They have been instructed to give them to your husband and only him; they'll get you through until you get yourself to treatment. Here are the phone numbers," he laid a sheet of paper on the side table, "it's up to you now. If you make the wrong choice, I don't know what to tell you except that you will not get any prescriptions from any doctors within a hundred miles of here." He paused and his eyes narrowed a little as he looked at me. "Good luck, Eileen!"

I knew he was angry. It would take the rest of my life to gain back the trust I had betrayed in everyone I knew. Then it all hit me. No one was going to baby me through this; the realization was so intense that my body stiffened, my jaw and fists clenched so tight it made my arms and neck ache. I didn't move from that position until Curt arrived an hour later.

He tried not to make eye contact with me; I continued to just stare.

"I'm in charge of your medication Eileen; there will be no alcohol in the house either."

I couldn't talk. I felt paralyzed again.

"Don't start this Eileen. I don't feel sorry for you; I'm going to tell you right now, don't start making promises to the girls that you're not going to keep. You are better off not saying anything about what is going to happen until you know for sure."

An overwhelming feeling of rage started traveling up my body, all the way from my feet to the top of my head and I started shaking again, my voice was loud and wobbly.

"I'm not making promises to you or anyone else," I screamed. "I know what I have to do, but there are some things you need to take care of also." I started to calm a little, my voice lowering a level, perhaps more out of exhaustion than anything. "I have the AA meeting schedule and I plan to go on Friday nights until I go into treatment… I'm not going to fight or argue with you until I leave," I said. "But I am leaving and I am not coming back until whatever has to happen happens." My face started to relax and the heat from my body started to subside. That was the first time I had spoken up for myself in many years. It felt good.

When we pulled up in front of our house the girls came running out yelling "she's home, she's home!" They were smiling and happy.

I got out of the car and ran to them. They both jumped on me and we fell onto the ground laughing and hugging and kissing each other. "I missed you two so much," I said with tears running down my face. "Let me just hold you both for a minute."

We sat quietly just holding each other. When we looked up at each other we were all crying; I looked over at Curt getting my things out of the car and he had tears running down his face as well.

The three of us sat in the front yard for awhile. Missy said "you look different this time, Mom. Why?"

Sara, excitable as she was, would have agreed with anything as long as it was positive, but she looked at me and said: "You do Mom, you look more awake."

The three of us started laughing. That day was a momentous occasion. I had begun my journey through hell. We had absolutely no idea what was ahead of us—especially me.

CHAPTER TWO

Early Childhood Memories

I don't see myself as a victim or an innocent bystander. I am responsible for all the choices I make. I am responsible for me, and my behaviors. To tell my story clearly, to relate my chosen road of alcohol and drug abuse, I need to go back to the beginning. My addictive behaviors started when I was a child. You see, the disease of alcoholism and addiction starts well before we pick up our first drug. My manipulation, self-destruction, pain, and lies started long ago.

I was the second oldest of eight children in a devout Irish Catholic family. We went to church every Sunday; I attended Catholic schools through my twelfth year; my parents drank—heavily. From my perspective we were the quintessential Irish-American, Catholic family—lots of kids, even more alcohol.

At one of the most important moments of my adult life, when I was just starting to get to know myself, I was asked to create a lifeline that started with my earliest memory. The goal was to note the ups and downs and connect them with a line. The good years would go up and the bad years would go down. Nervous as I was, I started to ponder my life, recollecting early memories and following through the years of my life to that moment in time. To my shame and embarrassment there were no up years that I could think of. The down years began right away. My first reaction was to lie and make up some good times. But I was at a place where I was putting all the lying and story telling behind me and trying to live honestly. Honesty—a totally foreign word to me. But, I was determined to get honest no matter how hard it was.

My earliest memory was from when I was four years old. My mother, father, and three of us kids had moved from New York to California where my father had taken a new job. We had been in California a short time, living in a temporary place before moving across the street to *the brown house*. I remember a big heater in the middle of the living room floor—the sole heater for the entire house, which made for many cold nights in the kids' rooms. I had woken up cold one morning and ran out to warm my feet on the heater. All I remember is screaming, unable to move, I stood frozen in place while my feet burned.

Hearing my screams, my father sprang from his bed and ran into the living room, he scooped me up quickly, but it was too late, bubbly blisters had formed on the bottoms of my tender young feet. To this day I remember the intensity of the burning sensation. Sadly, my timeline begins with a memory of physical pain.

Shortly afterward, we moved into the brown house. I loved that big house with its big dining room window, a built-in kitchen bench and a breakfast table. I remember it being on a very busy street that we never crossed without our parents. I was afraid of that street.

One of my clearest early memories is of my parents fighting. They screamed and yelled at each other as they moved from one end of the house to the other and finally out into the backyard. I screamed at them, pleading for them to stop. She hit him as he covered his head. I often tried to get in the middle of their fights; this would turn their anger toward me, which was a win for me—anything to make it stop.

I despised watching; every time it would start I would get a stomachache, my legs would start to shake, and my lips would quiver uncontrollably. Even when the fighting stopped, it would take some time before I would stop feeling afraid. My escape was sucking my thumb. I would run to my bedroom and hide under the covers. I had to hide it because if my mother caught me she would be angry.

I learned from an early age to hide from adversity.

Sometime neighbors would come over and stop them. Thank God for them.

The fighting became a regular occurrence in our house. It never felt normal to me, but it was all I knew. To this day, I can feel the pain in my stomach and the shaking in my legs—just writing about it brings me back to that place.

I was a crier when I was young. I cried every time their voices elevated. When they weren't fighting, I would study them, waiting, ready to prepare myself for all hell to break loose—it didn't lessen the pain.

Soon after we moved into the brown house, I started kindergarten.

I was very close with my younger sister of fifteen months. We looked like twins when we were little. While my older sister had already been in school two years, my younger sister and I were home alone with my mother every day. The job I gave myself was to make my mother happy during the day. That was impossible. In fact, I usually managed to do the exact opposite. I think she was relieved when it was time for me to start school. I was a hyper and talkative child; I just plain talked too much. The phrase I heard a lot was: "Eileen, calm down."

The first day of kindergarten came. I couldn't sleep the night before; I made myself sick from stress.

That morning my mother walked me down the street to the John Muir School. When we reached the bottom of the stairs to enter my school, I began screaming and crying, "please don't make me go, I don't want to go, I want to go home with you. Please," I cried and pleaded. I was sobbing hysterically. My mother took my hand and turned around, we walked back to the house in silence. She was not happy.

Finally she spoke: "You embarrassed me back there and don't you think I will forget it, young lady."

That night at the dinner table, my mother didn't mention my scene. Every day was the same; I would argue and throw a fit, we would walk home together and she would remain silent at the dinner table. To make matters worse, I made up stories of my day at school for my dad and sisters. My stories

27

were so exaggerated that no one believed them, but the family was getting used to Eileen's stories.

Then one night all hell broke loose. I heard my parents start to fight in the living room and I heard my name mentioned a few times. The fighting got worse and then the hitting and pushing started. I knew it was my fault. Beside myself with angst, I retreated to my bedroom; furiously I sucked my thumb until my teeth left impressions on my thumb and I started to bleed.

The next thing I knew, I could hear footsteps coming toward my room—it was my father. "You will go to school tomorrow and I will take you."

"Okay," I answered.

All night long I cried silently. My parents continued to fight and argue throughout the night. My mother came in to see me a few times "I hope you are happy," she had said with a look of hate and anger.

She hated me.

The next morning I got up and got ready by myself. No one said anything to me. I was sick to my stomach and my legs shook uncontrollably. My mother wouldn't kiss me goodbye when I went over to her, in fact she didn't even acknowledge me. So I walked out with my dad, he looked at me with that *I'm sorry, kid* look. He knew it hurt when she did that crap, which was all the time.

I decided that I would not be nice to anyone. I held back the tears so hard it hurt, until finally I could hold them no longer; my father was irritated with me.

"You can stop that crying," he said. "You are going to school."

"I know."

"You will have a ball; look, your teacher is waiting for you."

I could feel the teacher and all those kids glaring at me like I was part of a circus sideshow—they had witnessed my fits for the past week. I didn't imagine the teacher was too happy to see me.

I tried to put on a brave act for my dad, but I was scared to death. I don't know what I was so afraid of. Maybe I wasn't afraid; maybe I didn't want to leave my mother. All of my energy went into looking after her.

The teacher was nice at first, she tried to make me feel comfortable and asked if there was anything I would like to play with, but to all her questions I answered the same: "No thank you."

I turned and saw my dad still there watching me to make sure I was okay and I remember thinking to myself: *He does like me.* He saw that I saw him and a little panic ran across his face as if, *oh no she saw me*, but I ran over to him and said, "it's okay Dad, you can go now." He looked down at me and I saw something I had always looked for in both my parents' faces—to him it made a difference how I felt. So I gave him a kiss on the cheek and he left. There I was, surrounded by twenty or so other kids and yet somehow I felt alone.

I went to school every day. I hated it and got sick every day, but I went. Each night at dinner I would make up unbelievable stories. I told how the teacher liked me the best and how she had me do important things for her. Those were the things I saw happening to other kids, but at home I made them happen to me. In school I avoided people. I didn't want friends—or at least that was what I convinced myself. I just wanted to get each day over with and go home. If I had to be scolded by the teacher I would be devastated—more rejection. The color would go out of my face, and then I would turn red and start crying quietly. That is how I remember kindergarten, slow and painful.

My parents fought every night; I was convinced that they were fighting about something I had done. I would tell stories that I thought would make them think I was a good girl at school, maybe then they wouldn't fight. But no matter what I told them, they continued to fight.

Clearly I remember how my mother's face would change when my father would leave the house. It was a face that wasn't hers. "The look" we called it.

While I was young and vulnerable, I would ask her what was wrong. "Are you okay?" I would ask. "Can I help you do something? I can wash the dishes."

"No." She would snap back. "Shut up and leave me alone."

I would walk to my room and lay on my side so she couldn't see me soothing myself with my thumb.

The fighting worsened and turned violent. She would hit him until she thought he might hit her back and then would get in his face and scream: "Hit me! Go ahead and hit me!"

We kids would be right there crying and pleading for them to stop. Often we would run to our dad who would turn his attention toward us, "don't you worry," he would say, "I wouldn't hit your mother."

She would look at us with disgust and march away screaming obscenities.

The First Grade

Right about the time I was nearing the first grade, my mother's belly began to swell and she seemed to be happier. We girls were excited because we wanted a little brother. As it turned out, God had given us another baby sister.

I entered Holy Family just after she was born. We wore uniforms, which I remember liking a lot. But, still I didn't like the idea of leaving my mom alone all day. My older sister went with me and my younger sister, whom I adored, started kindergarten—I remember being worried about her. That was my lot—I worried about everyone and everything. My family called me "worry-wart."

I never was successful in school. I wanted to be; I wanted to succeed so much it hurt. I tried everything I could, but nothing worked. Later in life I learned that I had severe learning disabilities and ADHD, which answered a lot of questions, but it didn't take back any of the beatings I took from my mother for the bad report cards.

That night after my first day of school, my older sister played with the baby while I watched from the kitchen so I could see what was coming next—like it was my job. After a while my father came from the living room and said he was going for a walk. I was afraid he would never come back.

"Can I come with you?"

"No you stay here with your sisters. I'll be back."

I didn't believe him and I started to cry; I ran to the big window and watched him walk away. I wanted to be with him and make him feel better. Suddenly my mother's voice crashed into my silence: "What the hell are you crying about you big baby, baby, baby, baby!"

It scared me so much I jumped. I looked up and there she was with *the look!* She was bent over me, her face was so close to mine I could feel her breath and smell the cigarettes she had been smoking all day. She was screaming so loud she was spitting saliva on my face. *Oh God I am dead this time,* I thought.

"When are you going to mind your own business," she said as she brought her hand up and hit me across the top of my head so hard she knocked me onto the floor. I was stunned. I couldn't understand what she was saying while she was screaming. I just felt her spit and smelled her stink and it was making me nauseous.

I was both afraid and angry. I got up onto my knees and as I tried to stand up, she swung at me as hard as she could; she got me right in the back of the neck and I fell right back down onto the floor. My older sister came out yelling "stop it, leave her alone!" but she hit me again, this time I couldn't get up.

Everything was fuzzy, I could hear my sister and mother yelling at each other, but I couldn't make out what they were saying. My head and neck felt tingly and I heard someone coming up the front steps. I tried to get up, but I couldn't. The door swung open with a bang and my father rushed in.

"What the hell are you doing?" he yelled.

"Mind your own god-damn business," my mother yelled back. He ran over to my sister to see if she was okay and she told him that our mother kept hitting me in the face. In slow convulsive sobs I tried in vain to catch my breath.

He told me to go to my room, but I couldn't move. I was trying to tell him that, but he couldn't hear me over the yelling. That's when my sister helped me up and whispered for me to keep quiet.

She helped me into the bedroom and onto the bed. I felt like the room was spinning as we sat there in silence, listening to my parents fight for what felt like hours. I kept rubbing my neck and head, there was a bump on my head and a hard knot in my neck, but I didn't tell anyone. I didn't want to start any more trouble. There voices were getting lower so I thought they were making up, or at least talking nice to each other. All of a sudden the door opened and we jumped.

"What are you still doing awake? It's late you know."

No kidding I thought.

"Is everybody okay in here? No one got hurt tonight, did they?"

I spoke up fast, "No, Dad; nobody got hurt."

"Are you sure?"

"Yes. She was just mad at us."

"Okay, now go to sleep. It's very late and you have school tomorrow."

When he shut the door my sister looked at me and said: "You are not all right Eileen, she hit you hard and a lot of times, you should have told him."

But the fact was I didn't want them to start fighting again, I just wanted it to be over.

"Okay," she said. "Goodnight, Eileen." She slept in my bed that night. I felt so much better having her there.

The next morning everyone got up for school and I really did feel terrible, my neck hurt and my face was all puffy and my stomach hurt as usual, but I didn't say anything. It was hard moving my neck around but I faked it well. I got ready for school and went down for breakfast.

Everyone was in the kitchen. It was as if nothing had happened. My mother and I avoided looking at each other. I couldn't eat from the pain in my neck and throat. My father made a joke about me being so quiet and everyone just laughed. We were so tired from being up so late, but no one mentioned anything about it. I was angry and didn't want to go to school. I wanted to get out of it so bad but I didn't. I sure as hell didn't want to be home with my mother all day with my father gone; I was afraid of what she might do.

I had a terrible day at school. I didn't get the little bit of work she had given us to do the night before because of all the fighting and my teacher was very angry with me. I was the only one who didn't do it and to top it off she caught me falling asleep while we were supposed to be reading. She didn't like me at all and as far as she knew my home life was fine, she had met my mother who was wonderful and charming that first day of school—if she only knew.

That became the story of our lives. She sent me home with a note telling my parents of my behavior in school so I knew I was in big trouble—and just when my mother and father were getting along.

I was unusually quiet that night, but no one said anything. When my father got home we sat down to dinner.

"I have a note from my teacher," I said, but before I could get the sentence out I was crying.

"Go get it," he said. He did not say a word to me about any of it and never gave it to my mother and she never asked. "Tonight after the dishes are done I'm going to sit down with you and work on your schoolwork."

I remember feeling happy that he was going to spend time with me. But, it didn't turn out so good. He was very frustrated and upset with me—he ended up doing my homework for me and told me to go to bed. I felt horrible. That's how it always was, any attention I ever got was negative, and as always, I blamed myself.

From that day forward, when I would get home from school, my mother would ask me with a tone of condescension: "Do you have any notes?"

Some days I would. Some I wouldn't. She would send me to the kitchen with my books. I knew what I was in for. Before my father would get home, she would sit down with me. It was more how she did it than what she did that made me feel so bad. With a look of utter disgust she would spit and sneer as she made attempts to "teach" me; but of course she had no idea what I was learning in school. It was just a matter of time before she would get angry; if I didn't know an answer she would slam her fist down on the table and chastise me for being stupid.

Of course I got so nervous that if I did know what she was talking about I couldn't think to give her an answer anyway.

"Why are you so stupid? Your sisters don't have this problem. You don't pay attention," she would say, "that's what your problem is. I am sick of this! You'd better change your ways young lady—and fast, because from now on I am going to let your teacher handle you. I don't want any more notes. Do you understand?"

"Yes," I would answer.

"Watch your sisters. You might learn something."

It was true. They were very smart and I wasn't. I spent my entire life wishing I could be like them, or anyone else, I hated myself.

My learning years didn't get any better; the first grade was just the beginning.

The fighting between my parents just got worse, more violent, more hateful—more painful. Pain is the thing I felt the most as a child; it continued to haunt me throughout my life. It followed me through elementary school and into junior high; it followed me into every house we lived in, every relationship I ever had. I would later dedicate my life to hiding from that pain, finding ways to numb its presence and escape the powerful grip it had on me.

CHAPTER THREE

Discovering Childhood

We arrived in New York by train. It was a cold and snowy day. We kids had never seen snow before and we were pretty excited to get our first taste. Aside from the clothes on our backs and the sorrow in our hearts, we arrived empty-handed, ready to start a new life without our mother.

Initially we stayed with our Aunt and Uncle and two cousins until Dad could get us into a place of our own. He had taken on three jobs at once, doing anything and everything he could, anything that would pay him.

I remember they had a beautiful house. It was just right for four people—now they had nine more. My uncle, who was funny and always cracking jokes and making us laugh, made their attic into a dormitory with bunks and twin beds. It was wonderful. We had everything we needed up there, even a record player where we played Beatles records. I remember how the Beatles were just becoming famous and we couldn't hear them enough.

My aunt, who I thought was an angel, wanted all the girls to have everything they wanted, within reason of course. The months we spent living in their home were the best months of my life. My aunt was interested in what we had to say and she was a Girl Scout troop leader, so my sister and I were able to be girl scouts; we loved it. Living there we were able to experience things we had never imagined for ourselves. She made the time we spent with them so wonderful, there was no tension, no fear; we were finally able to just be kids and not worry. She bonded with the two youngest kids, they were just babies and she truly loved them.

I looked forward to coming home from school. I wasn't scared of what might happen when I got there. Although my cousins had never even met us, they shared everything with us, all eight of us.

I went to my first Easter egg hunt that year. My aunt took all of the children. I was so excited I remember my teeth kept chattering and I couldn't get them to stop. I vividly remember getting out of the car and seeing this beautiful park with so many colors and children everywhere—it was like a dream.

My aunt had planned a surprise party for my eleventh birthday that year. I had never had a birthday party before and I can't even explain the feeling it gave me—I actually felt important and special. She took time out of her busy, hectic life (that she had inherited from us) and threw a party just for me. No one had ever done anything like that for me before. Of course, she didn't even have to invite anyone because there were so many of us that we were our own party. But I was the star and the fact that my aunt cared enough about me to make me feel that happy meant the world to me.

Of course, my mother could not be outdone, she showed up the following day— unannounced. To this day my birthday gives me a dreadful feeling because it brings back memories of my mother. We had no idea she was in New York. Honestly, just the thought of her made me feel bad about myself and of life in general. I remember being in the bathtub and hearing the kids all yell "Mom's outside!"

She had come with her sister and asked my father if she could see me for a minute to give me a birthday present. I was sitting in that tub so confused, scared and shocked that she had used me as a reason for being there. For a minute I actually felt like she cared because she brought me a present. But my father came into the bathroom and said that I could not see her. I didn't want to see her but damn it, I wanted that present. I started crying, crying because I wanted something from my mother, crying because I knew my father thought I was being selfish, crying because I knew this new life we had been living was over. My father did the right thing. She had never given me anything before and there she was claiming to be there for me. Deep down, I knew it wasn't true.

It was bittersweet, that birthday; it gave me a glimpse of what it meant to be a child, but it also brought on a dread I've never been able to shake.

For those six months, I was almost a child, a happy, healthy, carefree child—almost.

A Light Went Out

On the last day of school that year, my father sat us down and had a talk with us.

"I've gotten a good job in Rochester," he said. "Along with a second job, so I'm going to be pretty busy. You know, kids, this isn't how I want things to be, but I have to do this to get us into our own home. So until then, because we can't put your aunt and uncle in this situation anymore, I've had to make a very difficult decision."

His voice started to crack and I got a pit in my stomach. I was scared for what he was going to say. I started to cry even before he told us.

"Until your mother gets the help she needs, and is ready to be with us, and I have enough money to get us a house and all the things we'll need, you'll need to split up and live in different homes for a short time. Each of you will stay with a member of the family; we'll try to put two of you together in each home.

"Your little brother and sister will stay here. I will be renting a room with a bed closer to my jobs. I will be working all day and in the evenings so I won't be able to see you for a while."

My world had officially ended.

No matter how horrible things ever had gotten, we had always been together. At the end of the day, I always knew that Dad was going to come home.

My mind started to race with so many emotions, I didn't know what to do; I didn't know where I would live. I was terrified.

"This is the only way for us to be together," he had said. "Eileen, I have to do this. It will only be for a short time."

I refused. "I don't care; I won't go." This was my usual response: refusal. All I felt inside was panic and anger. *Why is this happening? I can't live away from my father and my brothers and sisters.*

The day came to leave my aunt and uncle's. I couldn't stop crying. My aunt, uncle and cousins were sad too. But, this was our only choice, there were too many of us.

I don't deserve to be happy I had thought to myself. I knew that it was time for me to go back to feeling miserable and unhappy. It was like someone had switched the light off to my childhood, to my happiness. That was the day I lost hope.

My First Drink

My mother moved back in with us just before I entered the seventh grade. She turned angry and miserable very quickly after coming home. I was eleven that year—it marked my first experience with alcohol. My mother's sister would often come to visit and she always brought beer and liquor with her. I can remember watching them drink together; my mother would transform into an entirely different person—she laughed and smiled and had a great time. I don't remember her laughing at all when I was a kid.

There was usually beer in the refrigerator, so I would sneak it upstairs and drink it as fast as I could. I liked the feeling it gave me. I didn't even think I was doing anything that bad.

***

My mother often asked me to meet her at home for lunch; we were within walking distance of the school. I always knew I was in for it because I would be alone with her and the little ones. She would typically make me stay home the rest of the day.

I started menstruation that year. I didn't understand what was happening, but I was scared to tell anyone, so I hid my underwear under the cabinet in the bathroom.

She found them.

She didn't even give me a chance to take my coat off as I walked through the front door for lunch. She had that angry look on her face and I knew I was dead—of course I didn't know why. She clenched her lips and eyes as she told me to get up the stairs.

"What's wrong?" I pleaded. I started to cry. I was so scared.

"You make me sick," she said it very slowly as she moved in close until she was within an inch of my face. Then she grabbed me and threw me toward the steps; I fell against the wall as she yelled for me to get up.

I can see her face now, it was so angry and she spit as she spoke.

"You are disgusting," she yelled.

She came up behind me and started kicking me in the groin as hard as she could. I fell on the landing as I made a feeble attempt to hold my legs together. She continued to kick me over and over again.

"Spread your legs you whore," she yelled. "You disgust me!"

She grabbed me by the hair and dragged me up the stairs and into the middle of the bathroom where the dirty underwear were.

"What is this? What are you doing with that boy?"

I didn't know what she was talking about. She pushed me onto the floor and started kicking me again. She kicked me until I couldn't feel anything between my legs. I was crying and begging her to stop. I wanted to make eye contact with her so that maybe she could see how much pain I was in, but she wouldn't look at me. She didn't care. She finally stopped when one of the younger kids yelled from downstairs: "Mom, Mom, Mom."

She gave me one last kick and told me I was dirty and to stay away from her children. I just remained in the fetal position for who knows how long; I didn't understand what had happened. Of course there never had to be a reason for her going off, but I ended up having to see a doctor because of the bruising and a contusion I had between my legs—I didn't menstruate again for four years.

One of my sisters went through a similar confrontation with my mother—she ended up having surgery. The long list of physical abuse reached its peak and child services started coming to our home.

CHAPTER FOUR

An Addicts Perspective

Curtis is never home. I'm here all the time with Missy. I feel like such a terrible mother. I am. It's like a rat race trying to go to the doctor's and get all the medicine I need and keep up with my prescriptions. I take so many pills. God, I take so many pills. I have to stop taking so many. Doctor R. is acting annoyed with me lately and is starting to give me a hard time when I tell him I need more medication. I need to make an appointment with my baby doctor. I have the feeling I'm pregnant. I feel sick all the time. I can't eat. I didn't get sick with Missy, but they say every pregnancy is different. My legs hurt all the time. I have to stop drinking so much. I'm sick of having to hide it. Every day I tell myself I'm not going to have a drink until dinnertime. It never lasts, by lunchtime, if there's nothing in the house, I'm running to the store and getting enough beer and vodka to last a couple of days, but it doesn't last the day. Oh well. A lot of people I know drink during the day—especially if they have small kids. I'm doing what I can to get by. Today is no different than yesterday. It's three o'clock—I've been drinking since one thirty, as soon as Missy went down for her nap. She's going to be waking up pretty soon. It takes so much to even get buzzed. I've got to stop this.

It was another typical day. I had drawn all the curtains in the house to make it look like no one was home. I didn't want any visitors. I didn't want anyone to know what I was doing. I was hiding.

If there's nothing wrong with what I'm doing, then why do I hide it? I think about that when I'm drinking because then I start to get depressed and I tell myself how sad my life is. My husband is working two jobs. He cooks at a restaurant

and bar tends at night. He is never home. I don't think he
wants to be. He likes to play. He's always got something
going on. My life is horrible. I hate my life. I love being a
mom and I love my daughter, but I don't like myself too
much. I guess I'm taking about forty pills a day. I shouldn't
have to drink every day. But when I don't drink, I feel like I
have to have it. I can't make myself skip a day. I can't just
stop. I'm taking pain pills, tranquilizers, sleeping pills, and
antidepressants and any other mood-altering drug I can get
my hands on. Cocaine or crystal meth when I can get that. I
have been taking pills since I was seventeen years old. The
doctor said I was depressed. When I drink with them I get
drunk faster, but it takes more lately. If I'm pregnant I have
to cool it. That will be no problem. Maybe having another
baby will make me feel better.

I was very good at feeling sorry for myself. I would hide
myself from the world and think about my family. That was
a good way to instantly feel sorry for myself. My mother
wasn't speaking to me—as usual. She was always mad at
me. It had been that way since I was born.

It sucks really believing your own mother doesn't have
unconditional love for you when all I have to do is think
about Missy and she puts a smile on my face. She is the only
thing that makes me smile—besides getting high. I love her
so much and I felt that way since the moment she was born.
My mother has never looked at me with love. We don't even
make real eye contact with each other; we never did, not
even when I was little. I remember when I knew she was
angry about something I would look at her and try to get her
to look at me and she would get so aggravated she would
start screaming and telling me all the things she couldn't
stand about me, but she never did make eye contact with me.
That's ironic because my father is very blunt about always
making eye contact with people when you are talking to
them, or if they are talking to you. He always looked at me

when he talked. I was ashamed of the fact that my mother never really looked at me.

Well, I cannot stand the pain in my muscles. I cannot keep any food down. Everything I eat comes back up. I am exhausted all the time. I have no energy. I have to see the doctor. Maybe I'm pregnant. Curtis is not happy, which makes me so mad. He can't understand why I'm mad. "This is no time for you to have a baby, you are so messed up." I am messed up.

The rage between my husband and I would escalate and I would scream, throw every little thing I could get my hands on at him, and all the while Missy would be watching. Watching her parents fight, just like I used to do when I was a little girl.

The Guilt of an Addict

I was right. I was pregnant. Within a month I was in the hospital. My muscles were so weak that I couldn't use them. My potassium was so low; I was in a dangerous state. I had checked into a teaching hospital—one of the attending doctors asked me to participate in a question and answer class with the student doctors. They hadn't counted on my dishonesty. I wasn't about to tell them anything about my alcohol and drug use. Consequently they couldn't put the pieces together.

I stayed dishonest throughout my entire pregnancy; my husband enabled me by never speaking up or letting anyone no that I was taking thirty to forty pills a day and drinking every day. I would try and stop and after twenty-four hours I would get violently ill, and start sweating and shaking so I would have a drink and then slowly start taking the pain pills I had been given for the muscle pain. I had other pills that I had taken from people's medicine cabinets—at first I felt horrible about it, but then I justified it like I did everything else.

44

After awhile, the stealing—like the lying—got easy. I spent a lot of time crying and feeling the guilt of the harm I was causing my children, both born and unborn. The little life inside me was struggling, I knew it and yet I couldn't stop myself, so I would take more pills and cloud my guilt with a steady fog. I didn't know how to stop this horrible monster inside me. I cried every day but I didn't change anything. The closer I got to giving birth the more frightened I became.

We arranged for a specialist to be there—they still didn't know the truth. Writing about that time in my life makes me physically sick and I have to put the pen down for a while.

***

Sara was born sick and very small. There were substances in her blood—it was then that they began to see what had happened—I was confronted and told what kind of a person I was. I already knew what kind of a horrible person I had become.

I will never forgive myself for what I did. I had no right to take another human being's life into my hands and put her in danger. I look at her today and am so proud of the person she is and the obstacles she has overcome—without any crutches. She has ADHD and learning disabilities and yet she has been triumphant. She overcame everything with a positive attitude; even when she was in special education classes she was never embarrassed, she just took advantage of every opportunity she had. Her grades were outstanding; she and her sister were exceptional athletes and both got scholarships to college where they did wonderfully. They did it all without depending on easy fixes.

You would have thought when I finally got out of the hospital that I would have seen the light, that I would have finally gotten help. I didn't.

My husband looked the other way and I got worse. I couldn't deal with the truth. Every time I started to think about what I was doing, and what I needed to do, I would go into a fit, I would go crazy and lose control of my emotions and black out for days. My husband would care for the kids and the neighbors would help because they were wonderful people. They never knew the truth. No one did. But, everyone started to see what kind of a mother I was— neglectful and high all the time.

My resources had extended to many doctors. I would crash every once in a while and end up in a mental institution where all my problems were blamed on my childhood. Of course there were some very wise professionals who caught on and sent me to AA a few times, but I never kept up with that. I was in denial. I didn't believe that was my problem—I believed my mother was the root of all my problems. The fact is—I was the root of all my problems; my addiction was the cause of my very unhappy existence.

***

I would take at least ten or fifteen pills before dragging myself out of bed and making a feeble attempt to take care of my girls. My husband kept himself away most of the time. We had no relationship. Around noon the girls would take a nap and I would turn to the bottle and start drinking. Occasionally I would have a visitor who would come over and drink with me; the only friends I had at that time were fellow-alcoholics. I would pump myself full of pills all day long; it was a full-time job. Not a day would go by that I wasn't seeing a doctor or making an appointment to see another doctor. My day was consumed with taking and getting pills.

After a while I had to go out of town to get them because I didn't want the drug stores to start asking questions. My life went on like that for years. Sometimes I would accidentally overdose and end up in the hospital on a respirator. One night my husband came home from work to find me passed out on the floor. My oldest daughter was at a friend's house, but my baby was sitting over me crying hysterically—no one ever knew how long we had been there.

When I got to the hospital, they tried to pump my stomach but nothing would come up so they had to put a tube in me and give me shots to counteract the drugs I had taken. They injected me with something that would keep me from going into a coma, but the shots aggravated my system—I was in and out of consciousness and hysterics all the while yelling at the doctors.

That night the doctor said to my husband: "Your wife will never get better. She will die from this disease and you need to prepare yourself for that. She will never get better."

That stuck in my husband's head—it still does to this day. He says he will never forget those the way the doctor said it. Curt believed he was right.

My First Detox

Curt stayed with me all night and kept thinking about what the doctor had said. He thought about our daughters, and our life, and he began to see things for what they were. Sick. And it was getting worse. This addiction had such a hold over me—he knew he had to do something.

The next day when I came out of it, he said he had talked to the doctor and I would have to agree to get some kind of treatment, but first I had to be detoxed. They had a detox center at that hospital and I could be transferred as soon as I was able. I didn't like it and tried fighting him, but he wouldn't give in. In order for me to come home to the girls I had to go through detox first. I had no choice.

When I finally stabilized, they transferred me. I was not happy. I was scared. I felt like I had been beat up, my body ached all over. My tolerance for anything was low and I was mean to the staff. They gave me a rundown on what would be happening and that they would be there to control the withdrawal I would be going through.

I felt like hell. I was depressed. I wanted to get home to my girls.

As time went by I started to feel worse. I would sweat and shake and I experienced dreadful hallucinations. As soon as I would start to doze off, human-like figures would appear in the walls. They were very tall and thin and they resembled people I knew like my mother and other family members and they were yelling at me so loudly I couldn't stand the noise and I would wake up screaming. The nurses would give me a shot of Phenobarbital and that would help for a little while. But then the cramping and the vomiting would start again and all I could do was cry until it would let up. I couldn't stand to fall asleep because I would start to see things again—things I couldn't make out, but they felt like demons inside of my body that were trying to control me.

The worst part lasted about four days and then I slept about seven hours straight. When I finally woke up I felt better, but I was anxious and felt like I had to get out of there. So I waited until lunchtime because I knew the doors stayed open for twenty minutes so the staff could get in and out. There was only one person on the floor and she came in to give me my shot and commented on how much better I looked. When she walked out I ran to my door and watched her go into the office. There was no one else around so I made a mad dash for the door. I walked out and through the hospital and outside. Then I started to run toward my in-laws house, which was about fifteen minutes away.

Once I started running I became paranoid that they were following me, so I started hiding behind trees and bushes; then I sat down and started to cry uncontrollably for the first time since the whole process started. I felt like I was doing something wrong because I was. I knew I should have stayed, but I felt like I had to get to my girls or I would never see them again.

When I got to my in-laws house my girls were swimming in the backyard pool, so it gave me a minute to talk to my mother and father in-law. They were very supportive and understood my fears. I was crying and telling them I would do want they wanted me to do. They wanted me to go to an AA meeting. I agreed.

My sister in-law went with me. I was a nervous wreck. I was scared, I didn't know what to expect. It's difficult for me to remember what happened. I do remember being so surprised that my husband's family would go out of their way for me. I had never before asked for anyone's help. I did go to some meetings by myself after that, but before long I was drinking and soon after that I was doing drugs again.

I was a disappointment to everyone.

People from the AA group reached out to me, but I turned my back to them. I didn't want to stop using. I was depressed and didn't know it. I thought I was unhappy because I couldn't drink. My logic was screwed up.

I disappointed the people who meant the most to me and who did the most for me once again. My tolerance for the drugs and the alcohol was getting higher. I needed much more to even feel a buzz. That made it harder to get the pills I needed because I was taking so many. Drinking went right along with it. I never knew how my body would react, I could just as easily pass out or keep going strong and need more pills, more booze—I just couldn't get enough—it was scary.

I always managed to find some way to get what I needed. My speech by now had become slurry all the time. I never noticed it; I thought I acted just fine, which gave me a reason to take another drink or another pill. I would get up in the morning with the girls and try to take care of them, but half the time I would fall down the stairs. My body was so numb I wouldn't feel a thing. I had bruises everywhere and I made up lies about how I had gotten them. Anyone who knew me, knew what I was doing—they just didn't know to what extent.

The people who were trying to help were getting frustrated and mad. They knew I was taking drugs from their house, but never said anything to me. But now it was getting to the point that no one wanted me around. At the same time they were worried about the girls. I tried staying away from people as much as I could because I couldn't hide what I was doing anymore.

I had four more overdoses before I would get help for good. Each one was worse than the previous.

On that final day when I seized in front of Sara and my doctor finally knew the truth, I knew that was it. I had two choices, either die an addict and leave my children behind or kick drugs and alcohol for good. The truth had been waiting for me all along, but now it was out in the open and only I could save myself. I had to find a way to wallow my way out of the depths of my addiction, I didn't want to face it, but reality had hit hard.

I'll never forget coming home from the hospital after my final episode and seeing my girls with clear eyes. After spending what felt like hours in the front yard with Sara, Missy and Curt, I didn't want to move. Just watching the girls smiling and having so much to tell us was overwhelming for that one minute. They had not looked that content in years, or so it seemed to me. When Sara told me I looked more awake, we started laughing, but she was right, my eyes were usually half closed and I slurred my words from all the pills I took.

Sitting there on the lawn, I started to feel disgust for myself. What a horrible experience for my two beautiful daughters—the same experience I had experienced with my own mother.

I was starting to feel pain. Pain for my girls because I was putting them through a hell of their own. *What right do I have?* My own childhood started flashing in my mind and I didn't like one memory I was having—they all hurt.

I wanted to run for my pills, but the doctor had given Curt just enough medication to keep me from going into withdrawal before I could get into detox. He knew what I was in for. He had given me a schedule of AA meetings and fortunately for me there was one right behind my church, which was just up the street so I could walk there on Friday nights. Little did I know those meetings would have more of an impact on my life than anything I had ever experienced.

I had no idea what to expect. I was scared. I was more scared than anyone had known because as I looked at my daughters' beautiful and helpless faces, I knew that for the first time in my life, I had a lot of control over their happiness.

The Final Detox

The AA classes I had taken before detox were my first steps of preparation to stay the course. I was determined to make it work for my girls.

I was told I would be detoxed in one hospital and then transferred to another hospital for rehab. I didn't care; I had too much on my mind. My girls were staying seventy-five miles away with my father and I had no idea if I was going to live or die. I was going through withdrawal and I felt horrible. I was sweating and shaking, I had cramps in my stomach, and I had started vomiting the night before. The pills my doctor had given Curt weren't enough, my body was in a state of flux, my whole life was in a state of flux.

That morning I was packing and trying to follow the dress code for rehab. No alcohol company logos, no shorts— appropriate clothing.

I had a million things in my head. I kept thinking and stressing about never drinking again or being able to use pills to get me through each day.

What will I do? Will I ever have fun again?

The truth was, I had not experienced genuine fun for ten to fifteen years. I was in such a deep state of depression. My body was dying. I was dying. The seizures were burning my brain out. I couldn't control the shaking on the inside or the outside; my eyesight was failing and I felt sick all the time because my liver was so inflamed. I puked several times daily and was suffering from malnutrition. I was thirty-four-years-old, had lost my upper teeth and was wearing dentures already. I disgusted myself.

I was beginning to recollect painful memories I had buried with the drugs and alcohol, things I had been unable to deal with and bad choices I had made. The drugs were beginning to wear off and I was starting to feel. I was feeling pain.

On the way to the hospital, my husband gave me strict orders to keep his business out of it: "Don't discuss anything I do. You are the one that's sick. I function just fine—I go to work everyday, I take care of this family, you can't even get it together enough to leave the house."

I just sat in silence. I was scared to death and hurting from the physical pain I was going through. Suddenly I yelled for him to pull over.

He pulled the car to the side of the road and I barely made it out the door before I was bent over and vomiting repeatedly until my stomach became spastic and I had dry heaves. I got back in the car and I didn't have to say a word, I was shaking and sweating.

Curt put his hand on my shoulder, "I wish there was something I could do for you."

I started to cry. "There is nothing anyone can do for me now, I have destroyed my life and this is just the beginning."

"It's going to get better now. I wish you could see that, Eileen."

"Sure—I don't want to talk about it anymore." I was starting to get impatient and angry.

Before we went to the hospital, we went to see my friend Cindy who had been there for me. I had really hurt her. For the first time in my life I was doing something I had never done before—I was taking responsibility for myself. It wasn't easy. It was a behavior completely foreign to me.

I told her how truly sorry I was for hurting her and for scaring her with all my lies about my health. It was cruel what I had done. I explained that I was on my way to detox and then to rehab. "I know it will take a long time to trust me," I had said, I was sweating and shaking as I spoke.

She looked at me with tears in her eyes: "You just get well, Eileen."

We both started crying. That was the first time I had ever apologized for my drinking. She hugged me very tightly and I remember thinking *I don't deserve this. I don't deserve the forgiveness of anyone.* But, the fact was, she hadn't forgiven me, it would take her and a lot of people many years before they could forgive me—some never did.

I needed to do learn about forgiveness before I could understand it. I had a lot to learn.

When we got to the floor of the hospital where I would be staying, I felt extremely nervous and ashamed. Everyone knew why I was there. They probably thought I was a piece of dirt.

They were very professional though. I was taken to my room and asked how I was feeling.

"Horrible," was my only answer. And I looked horrible too; my belly was distended, but the rest of me was skin and bones. I was suffering from malnutrition, among other things.

Curt was asked to leave. "Bye," he said, "if you need anything, let me know."

I didn't respond.

"Let's go, Eileen. You don't look very well. Let's get you changed into a hospital gown. The doctor will be in soon to explain your treatment plan."

I agreed. I wanted them to give me something for the pain.

"The doctor will explain," was all she said.

This was not good. I was getting anxious. One of the nurses had to help me change my clothes. Another nurse came in with a clipboard full of questions. "I really don't have the patience for this," I had said.

"I'm sorry, but it has to be done. Answer the best you can. When was the last time you were medicated or had alcohol?"

"Last night. They were pills from my doctor, my husband was giving them to me."

"On an average, how many pills do you take in a day and how much alcohol do you consume?"

I hesitated, I didn't think she would believe me, but I decided to tell the truth. "About a hundred pills a day. Depending on what's available, I drink a bottle of whiskey or vodka and a couple twelve packs of beer—three if I can get more. Plus, any other hard liquor I can get a hold of."

I had to lie down at that point, I was dizzy and shaking and cold. I wanted blankets. Of course it was summer and it was warm in there, but I was freezing and sweating at the same time.

"When's the last time you ate?"

"I don't remember—I can't talk anymore," I said.

"Hang in there. Just a few more minutes; we have to talk about what you were doing and what kinds of drugs you were taking."

"Everything," I blurted out.

"Be specific."

"Oh God," I blurted out and then I began to list them as if subconsciously: "pain pills, tranquilizers of any kind, sleeping pills, antidepressants, amphetamines, pot, cocaine, muscle relaxants, crystal meth, anything that made me feel different."

The pills had stopped working. My tolerance level had gotten so high that I had truly been taking more than a hundred pills a day.

"I get confused," I said, "and can't remember what I've taken, or how many, so I just start taking over the counter drugs like Actifed, anything with the warning that it causes dizziness. I can't keep track of them."

It was so humiliating to tell someone that I had purposefully taken that many substances. I was beginning to feel worse. I started mumbling, I could hear myself talking, but I didn't know what I was saying. Then I started to see things. I thought I saw my daughters walking toward me from the far wall. The nurse must have realized how incoherent I had become because she offered to come back later.

I started to scream: "those are my girls!"

"No, your girls are not here, Eileen."

"They are too," I yelled. "They are right there," I pointed and shook my finger.

The nurses tried to soothe me, just as I began to settle down, I found myself running toward the bathroom where I heaved and purged the depths of my will into the toilet.

"I put a call into the doctor, Eileen, she'll be here to see you soon."

My regular doctor was on vacation, which I was glad for, because I was afraid to face him, afraid to face the truth and admit to the lies and manipulation that had kept me drugged for so many years.

I went back and forth between the bed and the bathroom floor where I battled severe cramps and ungodly vomiting. I started to wonder if it would ever end, my shaking and sweating was constant and eventually I was afraid to move from the bathroom floor.

The hallucinations persisted even though I knew they weren't real. I just kept telling myself: "it will go away, it will go away—please God, make it go away."

When the doctor on call finally came in, she told me they would not be giving me anything to ease the withdrawal because of the amount of drugs I had been taking. They were afraid I would have more seizures.

I started to cry. "You are not going to give me anything for the puking and diarrhea—nothing for the pain?" I was mad and my rage started to show through my tears.

Curt kept calling to see how I was, which made me angrier.

"What do you think?" I snapped.

I was mean and angry and sick as a dog—all I could think of was my need for relief. I wanted drugs. I wanted anything to make it easier. But, they were not playing that game as long as I was stable. They wanted my body to get rid of all the toxins on its own.

The last time Curt called, I yelled: "leave me the hell alone" and I threw the phone against the wall. He did.

My hours were cyclical, just as I would get settled under the covers and start to get warm I would have to run to the bathroom.

"Let me die, God!" I yelled form the cold bathroom tile, "please let me die—I can't do this."

I started banging my head on the bathroom wall. The nurses came in immediately and led me back to bed. My rage and anger was busting open. It was like they were trying to tame a wild animal. But when my anger would subside, my sadness would take over, and then came the tears.

"What a terrible person I am. I hate myself," I cried out loud. "My own parents couldn't love me—there must be something wrong with me," I told the nurses.

"No Eileen, there is something wrong with your parents—you are their daughter and through the good and the bad, we always love our children."

"Mine don't," I answered back. "I must be a horrible person. But I have to be better for my girls."

My mind started to play tricks on me—I kept imagining that terrible things were happening to my girls. *I have to get to my girls.* I got out of bed and tried running down the hall but the nurses on staff caught me and forcibly brought me back. I felt caged and enraged. But the rage was not just from that day—I was remembering things from my past, images of my mother's face laughing at me.

"Get her out of here please!" I was throwing my hands up trying to hit her, but she wasn't there. Everything was blurry. I was trying to move, but I couldn't. I started to sweat so much I was dripping wet, so they took me to the shower.

***

Later that night I called my father's house.

"Dad, can I please talk to the girls?"

He hesitated for a moment. "No, Eileen. I think it's better if you don't upset them."

"I am not going to upset them," I yelled.

"Listen to yourself. You are getting mad and they don't need to hear you like this."

I hung up the phone so hard I almost broke it. Then I called my husband and started screaming at him. He hung up on me. I was out of control.

***

I was lying in bed crying when the nurse walked in and told me she was taking my phone. "You are in no shape to be talking to anyone."

I ripped at my hair almost tearing it out I was so mad. "No you can't."

She didn't respond. They just left me alone to cry and get it out.

My regular doctor came into the room.

"Are you okay, Eileen?"

I just stared at him.

"You're lucky to be alive. I'm not happy with you. You nearly killed yourself. You manipulated me, and by the sounds of it, quite a few other doctors. I never saw it, you had me completely fooled and that scares me. Now I have to take a look at myself and rethink things when someone tells me they want medication, especially narcotics.

"You have taught me a few things, Eileen. When you are feeling better and working your program, I hope you will give me some time and educate me on this whole process."

"I don't feel good about lying to you," I said.

"This stuff right here will never happen again, okay?"

I shook my head and he came over and put his hand on mine, "you will get through this, but I am not giving you any drugs. I'm also taking the phone, it's not doing you or anyone else any good."

I felt deflated. I was so exhausted and worn out from the pain and the emotional rollercoaster I had been riding that I didn't care about anything.

***

The next morning I woke to the feeling of a volcano erupting inside me. After a night of tossing, turning, sweating, crying, and seeing images of my girls running away from me and my mother running after me—I started to feel something foreign. Something different was happening. I felt as if I would explode if I didn't get whatever was in there out of me.

My head was pounding with all those different thoughts and feelings, I tried to hold back the tears, but the harder I fought, the worse I felt. Fear, anger, regret, hate, and resentment were just a few of the feelings that were overwhelming my senses. I hadn't experienced those feelings since I was a little girl, back when everything made me cry.

As a little girl I was in so much pain; all I wanted was to be loved without feeling like I had to invent fantastic stories to get attention, or feeling so tied up in knots thinking about what I could do to make my parents just love me for me. That was impossible. I felt like everything I did was just not good enough.

When I learned to self-medicate and numb the pain, I realized that I didn't have to feel their rejection and I didn't have to feel my pain.

Twenty-five years later I found myself as a woman in a little girl's mind crying for myself, crying for my husband, and most of all, crying for my little girls. I was not going to let them feel pain and rejection one more day because I was going to change things.

I knew I had to be strong and take responsibility for my actions. I had to learn how to respect myself and how to be proud of me. It wouldn't matter how much rejection I had to deal with. It was now up to me. Emotions poured out of my being. It was impossible to distinguish the tears from the sweat.

"Are you okay?"

"No. I don't know what's wrong with me. I'm scared and mad and so sorry for everything I've done. What have I done to my kids and husband, my friends, and the people I've stolen from? Everything is coming back so quickly, all these feelings, I can't handle it, I can't stop crying. It hurts— it hurts so bad I can't stand it. I got to get out of here."

The nurse held my hand the entire time I was talking and when I looked at her, she had tears in her eyes.

"Oh God did I hurt you?" I asked her. "I am so sorry, I don't want to hurt anyone anymore. I don't want to hurt anyone else ever again."

"No it's okay," she said. "I am doing what you are doing right now, I am feeling my feelings. Right now my feelings are sympathy for you because I can feel the pain you are in. Eileen, this is just the beginning. I see hurt in your eyes. Can you talk about that?"

"I don't feel like I deserve to talk about my hurt because I should be hurting after all the things I have done to people."

"That is why you are here now, because of your pain. People abuse alcohol and drugs for a lot of different reasons. We believe you started long ago to cover up and even try to get rid of the pain you were dealing with when you were a little girl. Alcoholics stop maturing and growing emotionally when they start drinking or using drugs. Now that your mind is becoming a little clearer and sensitive, you will have to teach yourself how to deal with all those feelings— especially when so many feelings come at once. You will need a lot of counseling to teach you how to find positive ways to deal with it."

"So I am like picking up from where I left off? Scary."

"Don't worry. When you get to rehab they won't let you go home until you are ready and have learned everything there is to know about your disease. You'll have a whole new support system; they will be like a new family for you, people who have been there and have the same disease you have. They'll be there day and night and they truly care about how you're doing."

***

I fought hard to get through detox. After twenty-five years of taking excessive amounts of drugs and drinking daily, I was doing it—I was going to make it. *No matter what it takes, I can do it. Thank you God.*

The First Step

The morning I was to leave for rehab, Curt arrived late to pick me up. I had not slept the night before. I was still feeling sick and spent my nights sweating and vomiting, though not as severely as before. I felt paranoid and shaky and kept thinking that these feelings would never go away, which scared me to death.

It was obvious that Curt was impatient after arriving late—he had better things to do than take me to rehab. The first thing he said was: "You look terrible."

Before I could respond, the nurse standing next to me answered: "You would look terrible too if you had just gone through what Eileen has. We are very proud of her. Most people as sick as her would have given up, but she didn't. Not many people could endure the physical pain she is going through."

I was shocked. I just stared at her and said "thank you." No one had ever stood up for me before. She looked at me and saw the tears in my eyes, we hugged and I thanked her and the others for everything—mostly for their understanding. Curt stood quietly as he took it all in.

The doctor came in to see me before I left; he wished me the best and gave me the biggest hug: "I have learned a lot about addiction from you. I've never seen anyone as sick as you were. I hope you understand why we couldn't give you any medication. You are a fortunate woman—you should be dead. Be prepared to have physical problems from all the drugs and alcohol you have put in your body. You have caused yourself permanent damage."

I knew that, but I really didn't know how serious it was. That was just the beginning of my learning about the physical consequences of what I had inflicted upon myself.

We got in the car without saying anything to each other. I was in my own world—no one else was around as far as I was concerned, I was alone. It was as if I had just gotten off a long bender and had to face all the disgusting things I had done while I was in my drunken state.

I will never be happy—if there is such a thing. Maybe there isn't and everyone is walking around in their own miserable world.

Suddenly I heard Curt talking and reality hit. We were driving down the highway and he pulled out a joint from his shirt pocket. My face froze. He didn't even notice, he continued to tell me that I was the one with the problem. I was the one that had destroyed our lives because I didn't have any control and he was different because he went to work every day and supported his family and could function like a normal person.

"I am the one," he said, "that has sat in the hospital for days while you were hooked up to a dozen machines with tubes in your body and nobody knowing if you were going to live or die, I am the one that has come home repeatedly and found you passed out on the floor with our babies crying next to you—not knowing if you are dead or alive, I am the one that has cleaned you and the mess you make when you lose control of your bowels and kidneys, I am the one who covers for you when you have written bad checks or haven stolen drugs from someone else's house, and I get the phone calls from the girls when I'm at work and they are screaming because their mother is passed out and bleeding in the backyard because you fell out of the bathroom window, or they find you at the bottom of the cellar stairs because you're taking the house apart trying to find more pills or a can of beer you might have forgotten about.

"What do you think it's like for the girls and I to watch you go into horrible seizures because your brain is burned out, and finding you in the bathtub passed out in your own bodily fluids? What the hell do you think the girls think when they see this? For the past six months they have had to take care of you, help you get up the stairs because your body shakes so much and your legs give out and they have watched you fall down and almost kill yourself more times than we can count.

"Do I have to go on? Oh yeah, one more thing, the most important," he was yelling so loud my head was ringing, "you almost killed our girls before they were even born with the drinking and drugs while you were pregnant and now we have to watch our own daughter struggle with the problems she has as a result of you!"

I just stared at him—of course he couldn't look at me. I couldn't speak, but I remember getting on my hands and knees and begging him not to leave me when I found out about his affair. Who would take care of me? But he was right for the wrong reason; he knew he got me where it hurt the most. At that point I hated myself more than I ever had and it made me physically sick to think about all I had done.

"I don't want you telling these people that I smoke pot or drink, they don't need to know my business. I have put up with you and took care of you all these years and you better get help this time."

I started to fade away from the sound of his voice. *Am I hallucinating? Is this happening? Is he saying this? Is he really smoking that joint? Yes he is—I can smell every bit of it. I just went through over a week of hell trying to get this shit out of me and I'm still going through it and he is smoking pot.*

I felt the sweat running down my face and my stomach all rolled up in a tight ball and I wanted to scream in his face and tell him he was a selfish son-of-a-bitch and I detested him, but I couldn't open my mouth. I just sat there and kept my mouth shut and for the first time I couldn't wait till I got to rehab.

My feelings toward him at that time were hatred—I never wanted to see him again. As soon as we got there, they told him he had to leave; I couldn't look at him. I was so glad when he left.

They told him I would be in blackout for so many days and when I could call, and was ready, he would hear from me. I wasn't looking at him, but I heard him telling them what I needed and how to handle me. I shut my eyes and for the first time in fifteen years I really heard him and what he was saying and what he meant. I was disgusted with myself—this picture was my life. It made me sick. It took my mind off the anxiety of thinking about where I was and how bad I felt. I looked back at him as I was going through the door and thought to myself: *Curtis you are so full of shit.*

I wanted to say it out loud, but I couldn't. I look back on that moment today and realize that up until that point in our life together, I had always thought of us as being normal, but in reality we had been living a lie—we were dysfunctional as hell. I believe that I was starting to see it after spending that time suffering through a hell of my own making—things were becoming clear to me and I was starting to see things as they truly were.

***

They took me on a very quick tour of the floor and showed me where things were and introduced me to the counselors. I was given a schedule of the rest of the day and was told to go to group in the dining room. I was trembling and ready to puke. The fear of the unknown scared me the most.

I walked into the dining room to find a group of people sitting in chairs that formed a circle and everyone turned to look at me. I kept my head down and didn't look at anyone; I just sat down in a lonely chair that had been reserved for me. I sat sideways staring down at the floor. I was void of emotion. Mike, the counselor facilitating the group, introduced me, but I didn't say a word. The topic was feelings!

I knew nothing about feelings. To me you either felt good or you felt bad—that was it. Mike asked me how I was feeling and without looking at him I just replied "bad." Well that wasn't enough for him. Everyone was staring at me. I could feel their eyes burning a hole through me. Mike was waiting, he wanted an appropriate answer, but I had no idea what he was talking about.

"I don't want to hear 'bad,' " he said. "What is 'bad'? I want to know how you are feeling." His voice was getting louder and I felt a deep-seated fear overcome my senses; I didn't have an answer.

"I don't know what you mean, I answered you already. I feel bad. I am not happy to be here."

He started talking to the others and asked them to help me out.

"Take this paper and study it," he said as he handed me a piece of paper that had been torn out of his notebook with handwritten scribbles. "This is a list of feelings we all experience every day. I want you to study this until it makes some kind of sense to you."

I took the paper, but I didn't say a word.

"I think we need to talk about honesty," his voice rang loudly in my head as if he were yelling. I knew he was talking to me.

I continued sitting in the same position with my head down while they carried on their discussion. Again Mike asked me in a voice that was both loud and authoritative: "Eileen, how honest are you?"

I kept my head down. "I'm honest," I said in near whisper.

"Bullshit!" he yelled. "You don't lie to your husband or your children? How about your family, your brothers and sisters, your parents? What about your doctors? You had to get your prescriptions somehow. How did you do it, Eileen?"

I was so angry. He was telling everyone I took prescription drugs. I don't know what my expectations were, but I never thought there would be other people there who would end up knowing my entire story.

"Yes. I lied," I finally said.

"How can you say you're honest? You're not. In fact you're nothing but a liar and you know it."

He was really pushing my buttons. Suddenly I had enough courage to look up and stare him straight in the eyes.

"What's the matter, Eileen? Did I piss you off? You look really mad. I'm right, aren't I? You've never told the truth about anything to anyone probably since you were a kid and you know I'm right."

I felt like I was burning inside. I couldn't believe he was saying those things. And yet, no matter how angry I got, I couldn't respond. I was devastated. An entire room of complete strangers knew my secrets and they were all staring at me in utter silence.

"I have an assignment for you, Eileen," he finally said. "I want you to look up the definition of honesty and write an essay on how it pertains to you personally. I want to know what honesty means to you.

"Honesty is something we learn," he continued in a less angry sounding voice. "We are either honest or we are dishonest; but we don't just decide to be honest one day. As you will soon see, honesty starts within, once you start being honest with yourself, you might be able to be honest with the world." He stared intently at me as he spoke. I knew he was on to me, he knew I lied about Curt's drug and alcohol use. He stared at me with such a look of disgust that I was convinced he hated me.

Timidly I looked around at the other people; they were staring at me too. All of a sudden I felt panic-stricken.

What the hell is going on here? It's a conspiracy. They are all here just for me, just to get to me.

I wanted to run out and find the nurse who admitted me. I had lied about Curt—every answer I had given her was a lie. For the rest of the session, all I could think about was covering my face and hiding my shame. No one had ever talked to me about honesty before. I had never thought about it for that matter. Lying can be an addiction in itself. It was something that had come very easy to me. I had lied since I was a child, but I wasn't proud of it.

How the hell do I change it? I kept thinking to myself.

Before I knew it there was a hand on my shoulder and I was crying. I looked up to see the nurse standing over me. "I need you to come to the office and finish filling out your paperwork."

"Go ahead Eileen, you're done for now. I'll see you later." The look on his face gave me the chills.

I was so paranoid I could barely speak. I walked silently behind the nurse; her name was Libby. She brought me into a little room with a desk and a chair and gave me a folder. Then she left. I sat there in silence and cried for what seemed like hours but was only minutes.

What am I in for?

I was consumed with what might happen to me, no longer was I thinking about the chain of events that led me to that point. All I could think about was getting out of there. They were mean and I felt like there were cameras watching me in every room. I was so paranoid. I started filling out the paperwork, but it seemed like the same questions were being asked over and over again: How much alcohol did you drink? What kind of drugs? How many pills did you take? A little further into the questionnaire, I would see the same questions worded differently.

What is going on here? They must know I lied.

Suddenly I jerked up from my chair, throwing it backward into the wall behind me, and I bolted toward the door. I ran to the office with a look of complete panic that shocked the two or three counselors standing around the desk.

"I need to talk to Libby," I demanded. "Now. Please," lowering my voice to a more reasonable tone, "it's very important."

"Thank you. I thought you were demanding something, Eileen" Mike said.

"No I need to talk to her, that's all. It's very important," tears started streaming down my face.

Libby came out from another room and sat down in front of me. "What is it," she asked.

"I lied about everything I told you."

"What do you mean 'everything?'" She asked.

My stomach started churning and my palms felt wet and cold, my mouth had that dry feeling you get when fear is creeping in and taking over your senses. I knew I couldn't escape.

I better do what I am supposed to, I was thinking to myself. *These people are not messing around.*

Libby must have noticed my fear because her voice softened a little.

"I lied to you about everything I ever told you about... my husband... the things he does and our relationship. He drinks just about every day and he has done a lot of the drugs I did and he lives on marijuana... he has to smoke it every day he has been doing that since he was a kid. He didn't take any prescriptions drugs like I did and he went to work every day so he told me not to tell you guys about him because I was the one dying and I am the one that has ruined our family and on the way here he smoked a joint knowing I was still in withdrawal and what I had been through.

"I was so mad at him I wanted to kill him, but I never say anything, I just do what he tells me to do when it comes to this stuff. He has had a lot of affairs and I just found out about them recently. I know everybody thinks he is a saint for putting up with my crap, but he is no saint." I felt myself unraveling as the words poured out of me. "I'm scared. I don't want to see him while I'm here and I do not want to talk to him. All he will want to know is if I said anything about him."

"I couldn't wait to get away from him today. I was relieved when we got here and he had to go...." I was hysterical by now, but Libby was doing her best to comfort me.

"We know this, Eileen. Calm down, it's going to be okay, but this is in your hands. Only you can decide what you want. We will respect your wishes, if you don't want him to call, he won't—or at least he won't be able to talk to you.

"You are in blackout now anyway so stop thinking about him. I'm really glad you are being honest about this. You just made your first attempt at getting sober and I am proud of you."

She went to the door and motioned for another counselor.

"Eileen is having a hard time right now she thinks she is losing control, but she's just upset."

"I have to get out of here," I blurted out, panic was creeping in again.

"There is another session in fifteen minutes," she said. "That's just what you need, you are feeling a little anxiety, but it will pass."

I was beginning to realize that no one was going to coddle or baby me. There was no feeling sorry for myself, and no way I could manipulate these people, it was clear that they had seen every trick in the book, and I was no exception.

They didn't react to my confessions; in fact they seemed to have expected it—as if they already knew the truth. I was blown away.

On the way to the next session, I met the director of the floor, he was emotionless like everyone else. It seemed to me that everyone I had met was either placid or angry, there was no in between—I was not going to be making any friends, that much I knew.

As I walked into the next group session, everyone looked up at me. I tried to slip in quietly with my head down. But the counselor, Tony, immediately acknowledged me and gave me two books and several empty notebooks for my assignments, of which there would be many.

"These books are the most important things you will have in your possession while you are here and after you leave," he explained. "I know you're familiar with AA so you must know or at least have heard of the twelve steps and twelve principles of the program. Read them every chance you get."

He instructed me to sit down and listen. They were discussing the First Step.

"Who would like to explain the First Step to Eileen?"

A young man who didn't look a day older than eighteen stood and spoke: "I admitted I was powerless over alcohol and my life was unmanageable. I accept that I am an alcoholic and a drug addict." He seemed so young to be battling addiction. They had told me that addiction and alcoholism does not pick or choose its victims, it just takes— I was beginning to believe it.

I spent the next twenty minutes in my own head, consumed with one thought: *I am powerless over alcohol and my life is unmanageable.* I kept repeating it to myself, and the more I did, the more anxious and out of control I started to feel. Finally I tried to focus on the group and to my surprise Tony was trying to get my attention. "I'm sorry," I said. "I was thinking about the first step."

"Good," he answered. "That is what you're supposed to be doing, but you also have to participate in the discussion," he paused for a moment and then asked me: "What does it mean to be powerless over something?"

"I guess it's not being able to do something."

"That's all? Not being able to do something?" He spoke with a loud and intimidating voice. "You can't come up with anything better than that?"

I noticeably jumped in my chair and immediately started to cry.

"You're crying?" he asked with an ironic tone. "Why are you crying?"

I just sat there looking down.

"Why are you crying?" he repeated more harshly.

"I don't know." I whispered. "You scared me."

"I scared you. Did it scare you when you overdosed or when you put yourself in intensive care time after time? Did it scare you when you were falling down drunk in front of your kids and they were looking at you crying because they were afraid of Mommy?"

I just stared at him with hatred. I wanted to tell him to go to hell. But I didn't have the guts and he knew it.

"Was your life unmanageable?" he asked.

"I guess so."

"You guess so? You don't know?"

I started screaming "I don't know, I don't know, I don't know. Why is everyone so mad at me? What the hell is going on in this place? I want to go home now."

"Of course you do. Is it getting too tough for you?" He asked with a condescending tone. "When things get tough you want to run and hide, don't you? Well, that's going to change. We are going to break you down and build you back up."

I was scared to death. *This isn't right, what are they going to do to me?*

"I want you to read about the first step in the big book and then write an essay on what it means to you, but not until you are done reading."

I nodded my head.

"What does that mean?" he asked.

"Yes. All right. Yes, I will do it." I didn't understand why he wasn't addressing anyone else, but I wasn't going to ask either.

Making It on My Own

I was relieved to get to my room. I just sat on my bed and stared, my mind moving at a million miles an hour. *I don't believe this. I didn't expect this. I don't understand.*

Just then my roommate walked in. "You had it hard today," she said. "I've never seen them be that hard on someone. You must have done something. Whatever you do, don't let them see you sitting around doing nothing—that'll make 'em mad for sure."

"What are they doing to me?" I asked.

"They aren't doing anything to you. It's for you; this is the only way us alcoholics seem to understand what the hell we are doing to our lives and everyone else. They knock us down and strip us of everything and then build us back up. This will be my fourth week here so I am starting to understand it. It works. I want to stay sober when I leave here—I hope I can do it."

Her words kept repeating in my head. I decided to take her advice and took my books to the dining room and sat down to read. The anxiety of having to write an essay was overwhelming.

Dinner that night was handled as if we were one big family, everyone participated in some way and we all sat down together. That was new to me because even though I had always fixed dinner for my girls, I had done it out of guilt. Rehab was becoming a constant reminder of all the bad things I had done and all the things I would have to make up for.

I met more people that evening, but I felt nervous and ashamed even though they were in there for the same reason as me. Paranoia consumed me, I was convinced that cameras were watching and listening to our every move. I couldn't figure out how they knew so much about me and knew what I was thinking when I was thinking it.

My anxiety continued. I felt overwhelmed by the need to get out of there, but I knew that was impossible, so I snuck off to my room to be alone and cry.

"What are you doing?" It was Stan, one of the male counselors. He had caught me. "You do know you are not to be in your room until bedtime don't you? You've been crying haven't you? Is that a regular thing with you? Crying?" He asked sarcastically.

"No it's not a regular thing. In fact," I said, "it's not a thing for me at all. I stopped crying years ago, I couldn't cry, but ever since this whole thing started I feel like I am crying all the time. I hate it. It hurts."

"It hurts does it? That is a feeling; hurt is a feeling. Did you know that?"

"No, but I don't like it—it pisses me off." I was crying again, I felt like I couldn't stop.

"So crying is not your thing? Well I got news for you, you're going to be doing a lot of things that hurt in the next couple of months because you're not self-medicating anymore, no mood-altering drugs to control your hurt.

"From now on, when someone gets mad at you, or happy with you, or gives you bad news, you are going to feel it. It's okay to smile, or be sad and cry if something hurts. Baby steps. First you need to work on your tone of voice and you have to make eye contact with people, whether you are talking or being talked to." He was stern and serious.

"Let me tell you how others perceive you Eileen, you don't stand up straight, you lean on one leg with your shoulders hunched over, and your head down—it appears that you talk with your eyes closed, you mumble when you speak. I want to see you stand up tall, shoulders back, look at me. Speak to me so I can hear you. Do you understand?

"Crying is perfectly normal. I hope you learn that it's okay to cry, it's not a sign of weakness, which I am sure you have been taught. In time you will learn when it's appropriate and not. Am I clear?"

"Yes," I answered.

"What?"

I looked up and put my feet together, I tried to look him in the eye, but I was shaking so much, I just said yes again, but in a louder voice.

"When anyone here is experiencing an overwhelming feeling there is a bell right over here on this table, you are to pick it up and ring it. When the rest of the group hears the bell everyone goes into the conference room and sits down. The person who rang the bell sits in front, facing everyone, and shares what they are feeling. It doesn't have to be a sad or upsetting feeling, it could be something nice or happy that has happened. The group is here to support you and give you feedback to help deal with your feelings.

"That's how we learn to support each other and be there for each other. We are in this together, day and night, and we need to reach out. I'm sure you can't remember when the last time you admitted that you needed something or someone. Right?"

Down went my head and quietly I said: "Yes, I don't ask anyone for anything."

"You don't get hurt that way Eileen. I know that game."

We stood there in silence for what seemed like an eternity until he said: "You have an AA meeting now, I want you to listen real well."

Of course I walked away crying. My eyes were puffy and red, but I didn't care what anyone thought. I was more concerned about all the crying I was doing. There were a few people coming in for the meeting. A woman just a few years younger than me caught my attention. She was smiling and talking to everyone and asking how everyone was doing. *Why is she so happy?* I asked myself. She had to have been an alcoholic or she wouldn't have been there.

I wanted to be able to laugh and smile, but it seemed so impossible. I found an empty chair and sat down away from everyone, but the room quickly filled to capacity.

Though I was familiar with AA meetings by this time, this meeting was a little different for me. I related to at least one thing each person had to say. Learning why other people were there was a big help for me.

The same haunting, stabbing secret had been going through my head since I arrived: my daughters and the fact that I drank so heavily while I was pregnant with them and that Sara suffers the most from my added drug use. I despise myself for those things. Nothing could be worse than hurting an innocent child. I was now becoming aware of that pain and the feeling of self-hatred was growing deeper daily.

Of course, using would take care of the immediate pain, but it wouldn't take care of the everlasting pain we both suffered. I knew I had to stay and face my demons. Listening to the stories of those around me and the things they had put themselves through helped me believe that maybe I could do it too. I was not alone. I never would have believed it had I not hit bottom. There were people living with the same pain and shame that I had been living with for twenty-five years.

By the time the meeting ended, I was so glad I had been there. I heard so many things that I had thought or done and I didn't feel alone anymore. It didn't make anything better, but I decided I would try harder to listen and learn. After the meeting people started going up to each other and talking and hugging. I wanted to talk to the woman who had chaired the meeting, but I just stood still and watched. Finally I turned and walked out of the room; I couldn't bring myself to approach anyone.

I didn't know what to do next, it was a small place with no space for privacy and I knew I wasn't supposed to go back to my room. I started to feel panicky again when I heard a voice behind me: "Well, what did you think of the meeting?"

A female counselor stood behind me with a stern look of inquiry on her face; she was the tough one. I was scared of her.

"I liked it," I answered.

"What did you like about it?"

"I'm not the only person who has done the things I've done, and yet..." I paused and put my head down. Pangs of guilt hit me hard and made my heart feel like a sinking brick. "I know I've done something so horrible that probably no one here has done it."

"Sounds like you have some important things to discuss with your primary," she said as she walked away. I was relieved. My heart was beating so fast I had to go to the restroom to calm down. Everywhere I turned there was someone there to remind me of what a horrible person I was.

After lights out was announced, I made my way back to my room and crawled into what would be my bed for the next few months. My roommate came in and started talking to me.

"You are really freaked out aren't you?" she asked me. "Or are you always this introverted? I know dope and booze will do that to a person—it just takes all your personality and flushes it right down the toilet."

"I'm not as freaked out as I was earlier," I said. "I miss my girls. I don't like talking to people anymore, it's gotten worse the last couple of years."

"You will learn all about what this disease does to your mind and body while you are here. It'll scare the shit right out of you, but every bit of it is true. I go home tomorrow and right now I am determined to stay sober; I have a lot to lose if I don't. I have screwed up a lot of people's lives."

"I have broken my daughter's hearts a million times over," I sympathized. I then sat and listened to every word she had to say. She was scared to go, she felt secure in there and knew that getting out meant having to face all the temptations and realities of life. That really hit me hard. I didn't sleep at all the first night, I just kept thinking about those words.

What will my life be like after this?

***

The next morning we got up early and started with breakfast. It was Tuesday, floor meeting day with the patients and the director. Everyone was given a job for the week. One of us would be appointed floor monitor to make sure all the jobs were done and done right. I did not want that job—I knew I would die if I had to criticize other people's work or tell them what to do. I started praying as soon as I heard about that, that I would not get that job.

Jobs were to be appointed after lunch.

I was called down to the main desk, which made me think the worst. It turned out that my primary counselor wanted to see me. I was relieved.

"She is in that office," someone said, as she pointed me in the right direction, though I didn't see where she was pointing.

"I turned and walked into the first door I saw—thank God it was her office. She stood and introduced herself and told me to sit down.

I sat there while she looked over my papers. "You had a quiet day yesterday, you didn't talk to anyone," she said. "Well, that will change."

My heart started to thud rapidly in my chest. I was worried she might hear it.

"Eileen." She looked me straight in the eye. "This disease has taken your personality—I can tell just by looking at you and your body language. I want you to sit up straight and make eye contact with me when I am talking to you, even if I am not talking to you. Look at me."

"Okay," I said timidly.

She just stared at me. "You are damn lucky you are alive. One hundred pills or more and booze every day. You are here for a reason and it may take your whole life to find out what it is, but you should be grateful. You are a miracle. I was just reading about all your physical problems. We're gonna have to watch you closely. How do you feel right now?"

"Not very good, dizzy and sweaty. I didn't sleep at all last night, in fact I haven't slept since that night."

"The night of the seizure, I assume. I see your daughters have been taking care of you. You are going to have it tough when you get home. I hope you realize that."

"Yes." The tears started again and I felt a terrifying feeling of helplessness.

"I would be crying too if I were you, but if you work on your program and listen, things will change for you—not immediately, but you will begin to see a consistent change. I'm willing to bet that you haven't done a lot of crying in years and now you can't stop. I am going to tell you why.

"You have been numbing yourself with booze and drugs for twenty-some years so you haven't allowed yourself to feel any feelings. I see you were discussing feelings in group yesterday and you didn't know a lot about that subject. You said you either feel good or bad.

"Now I am going to give you this sheet of paper, it's full of the different feelings we experience during a day. Feelings are not what will hurt you, burying them deep down is what will hurt you and that is what you are feeling right now. All the feelings that have been bottled up inside of you are screaming to come out and they are slowly coming to the surface. That's why you feel like crying all the time. All the things you have done during your active addiction that you couldn't face are also coming to surface. Am I right?"

"Yes," I answered. "I feel so guilty about so many things, some of them I can't talk about. I'm too afraid."

"Well maybe those things aren't ready to be dealt with yet, but they will. Just don't stuff them. Let them come to the surface. Cry over them, scream about them, ring the bell if you have to, but do not stuff them.

"The fifth step says: 'We admit to God and another human being the exact nature of our wrongs.' I don't want you worrying about this now, but before you leave, you will have completed the fifth step. You may choose a priest or someone else you feel comfortable with, but you will tell that person all those things you can't tell anyone else right now, maybe never, but this will help you face those wrongs and feel them. No more hiding. That part of your life is over as long as you work your program and go to meetings. You will also learn about getting a sponsor when you leave here. That is someone in the program you have met who has some good sobriety under their belt, someone you can relate to.

"Take your time and choose someone you feel you can trust. One thing we do ask is that you stick with the women. Males stick with males and females with females. It's better for everyone. You are in a vulnerable place right now and you don't want anything confusing that. Is that clear?"

"Yes."

"I see that there are some issues with your husband and you don't want to see him even when your blackout is over. That's okay. You don't need anything or anyone influencing you right now. The people you need are right here. I have given you a lot to think about today so what I want you to do is start mixing with the other patients, find out something about someone and tell me about it tomorrow. No more isolating. Isolation is a setup for relapse. Talk to people. Get to know them, you might find out something you need to know. Okay?"

"Yes, okay. You want me to talk to someone before I see you the next time, right?"

"Yes, I guess you could put it that way. I believe there is a group session going on right now so you should get going; I don't want you to miss it. We'll meet tomorrow. Have a good day. And Eileen, let yourself cry. It's okay."

"Okay, thank you." I walked out of there and took a deep breath. *Well now I know why I want to cry all the time. She knew just what I was thinking—I have so many secrets sometimes I just want to scream.*

***

The session I joined was on the educational part of the disease, of alcoholism and addiction. I only missed the first five minutes. I saw everyone else was taking notes so I took out my notebook and started listening.

The Gripping Reality of Alcoholism

The counselor was teaching statistics on the disease of alcoholism: "Fifty-three percent of men and women in the U.S. report that one or more of their close relatives have a drinking problem. The four symptoms of alcoholism are:

1. Craving, a strong need to drink.

2. Loss of control, the inability to limit your drinking on any occasion.

3. Physical dependence, withdrawal symptoms start when alcohol use is stopped.

4. Tolerance, the need to drink greater amounts of alcohol to get high.

"Non-alcoholics don't understand why an alcoholic just can't stop, or use just a little and then stop. They believe it is due to a lack of willpower. Alcoholism has nothing to do with willpower. Alcoholics are in the grip of a powerful craving or uncontrollable need. This need is as strong as the need for food and water.

"Many people wonder why some of us can use alcohol without problems and others cannot. Genetics is one big reason. Having an alcoholic family member makes it more likely that if you choose to drink, you too may develop alcoholism. Genes are not the whole story, they have found that one's environment will influence whether a person with a genetic risk for the disease will develop alcoholism.

"Alcohol abuse is different from alcoholism and does not come with that strong craving for alcohol, loss of control, or physical dependence. Alcohol abuse is defined as a pattern of drinking that results in situations such as: failure to work, go to school, or take care of personal and family responsibilities; drinking in situations that are physically dangerous such as driving a car; having alcohol-related legal problems and continuing to drink during relationship problems caused by drinking.

"Alcohol abuse is different from alcoholism, but the effects of abuse are also experienced by alcoholics."

He continued to relay these facts to us and told us that our children were genetically at risk of becoming alcoholics too, especially if one or more of our parents or other relatives were alcoholics. I got very upset when I heard this because there is a long line of alcoholism in both my parents' families.

I started to cry, I felt the counselor's eyes on me, but he said nothing—thank God. I was thinking of my girls, my innocent girls whom were only ten and eight years old. Their self-worth and self-confidence had been damaged not to mention a lot of other things. Missy had taken on the role of parent, while Sara had become the caretaker—she made it her job to make everyone happy. Sara's addictive tendencies had already been triggered from fetal alcohol syndrome that I caused while carrying her.

In our society there is the myth that an alcohol-related problem is a sign of moral weakness, I had to believe right then that if that were true, I would not be in treatment. Before that day I had believed in that moral weakness, had it not been for my failing health I would not have sought treatment on my own. I fought it to the bitter end when I was told I would die or get treatment.

Suddenly, at that moment, I realized that it was not a moral weakness and that some things were beyond my control. After two days in treatment, I was beginning to see alcoholism for what it is—a disease that leaves you powerless.

Finding My Power

There is no cure for alcoholism, but you can remain in recovery as long as you work on yourself. Relapse is another real part of the disease. Relapse should not be looked on as failure, because it is just another stage, and recovery is always possible. Every day that a recovering alcoholic stays sober prior to a relapse is extremely valuable time to the individual and their family. A relapse just means that that person needs support in order to abstain from drinking. Research continues for new addiction treatments. Luckily, and perhaps ironically, there are now medications to help treat the disease.

I felt pretty beat down after that session. All I could think about was that my daughters hadn't gotten a fair chance in life. The counselor pulled me aside afterward and asked me what had bothered me the most. I told him how I felt about my girls and their chances at getting or already having the disease.

"I understand your concern," he said. "The only way you can prevent that from happening is to not drink and continue to go to meetings, educate them and show through example how staying sober saved your life."

A light bulb went off in my head.

"Are you okay, Eileen?"

"Yes." I stammered. "I can't believe what just happened to me, just then, it's like now I get it. I have to stay sober. I have no other choice and that's okay, it's for the sake of my children." I was crying.

"You will always have a choice. It's the choice you make that will make the difference in your life."

I went to my room knowing I wasn't supposed to be there. I didn't know what else to do, I couldn't stop crying and these were different tears, these tears were intense tears. On the one hand they were heartbreaking, but on the other they were good tears. I think I got it. I buried my face in my pillow so I wouldn't make so much noise.

This Too Will Pass

Every day was different. I was learning new things about myself and about life. I was learning to live life on life's terms without drinking or drugging. It was scary, but I was determined to do it, if not for me, then for my girls.

It was the first time in my life I hadn't been medicated out of my mind and it was amazing. We were allowed to go outside every morning for an hour of exercise, but that was it. Every moment was dedicated to staying sober.

Everything that has happened to me from that time on has helped me grow spiritually. I do not believe in coincidence, things happen because God wants them to happen. In AA there were many slogans like "let go and let God," "one day at a time," "this too will pass," and many others that at first had no meaning for me, but soon helped me to keep things is perspective and stay focused on staying sober.

***

The first time I talked to Curtis I was told by one of the counselors that it was going to be up to me to tell him that I wasn't ready to see him yet. That did not go over well. He couldn't understand why. I told him I wasn't ready. He was shocked, and so was I.

Who the hell did I think I was? He reminded me that he had been taking care of our children and doing everything so I could be there. He was making it all happen for me and I had better remember that.

"No, I'm making this happen for me," I said, "and you need to know that I am doing all the work and you need to take a good look at your own alcohol and drug use."

"Oh really? Now I have a problem? You better remember that you're the one that has caused all the problems in this family. You made the girls a mess," his voice was getting louder and he was getting mad. How dare I tell him I wasn't ready to sce him? He was the one that should decide if he wanted to see me or not.

"Well obviously you do want to see me or you wouldn't be getting mad because I'm not ready yet"

"Eileen, I'm the one who has to get all new furniture because you have ruined everything by puking and shitting all over everything we own. The girls and I have changed all the curtains and all the comforters in the bedrooms so everything will look nice when you come home and you have the nerve to tell me you don't want to see me."

"What do you mean you have changed everything? I know what I have done to our home and believe me, for the first time in my life I am feeling some embarrassment and remorse, but as far as the curtains and any redecorating, I would have liked the pleasure of doing that myself. You have been doing things like that for years, right up to choosing and buying my clothes and that is going to end. I am going to do those things for myself. I am an adult. I appreciate the fact that when I couldn't do those things you did it for me and I always will, but now I am sober and I want to take care of myself and make my own decisions. I don't want anyone making them for me anymore."

"You are being blackmailed, I don't know what those people are telling you, but this is not you, it is someone they are making you into, and I don't like it and I am coming there tomorrow and taking you home."

"You are not. I am sober. This is me talking and you aren't used to it, but this is the way it is going to be. I would think you would like it this way. Aren't you sick of taking care of me? I would like you to do me a favor if you would? Bring me a couple of pair of jeans. I guess I am going to be here longer than I thought, okay?"

"You are kidding? Longer? I need you home to take care of the kids. I have to take them to the babysitter every day and go to work, I want things back the way they were, you need to get home and take care of the kids. I have been working my ass off."

"I am sorry, but this is how it's going to be, now are you going to bring me those things or should I call someone else?"

"No I'll drop them off tomorrow and don't worry, I won't ask to see you."

He slammed the phone right in my ear. He was so angry and it scared me, I had never stood up to him in that way before and both of us were in shock. But for the first time I heard what an ass he was.

Already I knew there were going to be some major changes in my life. I also knew my crying was due to the fact that I was no longer masking my feelings with medication. I now was going to start experiencing life on life's terms. I had never dealt with or faced anything head on before. I really needed to learn to live one day at a time or fifteen minutes at a time, which was about all I could handle at once.

Slowly I started to take part in group sessions and became more vocal during my one-on-one sessions with my primary counselor. I started talking about my issues, which was very uncomfortable, but I learned to accept constructive criticism as well as confrontation. I was beginning to let people in and almost trusting them with my life.

Curt brought the clothes. He asked to see me, but he was told that visiting hours were only on Sundays and I had not allowed Curt on my visitor's list. I had no one on my list. He got angry and started saying I was being brainwashed and turned against him.

"She is my wife and I want to talk to her now." He got no reaction from Mr. D. and he realized he was getting nowhere. He also knew he needed a friend up there so he changed his tune fast and asked if he could see me for a minute. That was impossible. The rules were not going to be broken for him. He knew he was not going to get what he wanted and that was something he wasn't used to, but he had no choice. "What do I do to help her and support her? I want to see her."

"I know you do but first she has to request you on her list and when that happens you should come by yourself, you two have things to talk about. But it is your decision what you do and how you do it."

Curt shed a tear or two, but it had no effect on Mr. D., who was used to manipulation. He saw right through my husband. Then Curt asked if the counselor would encourage me to see him.

"That is Eileen's decision, she is quite capable of making her own decisions."

"You don't know her, she needs a lot of help and sometimes you need to tell her what the right thing to do is."

Well that did it. "You'll be surprised when you see Eileen, she is capable of making her own decisions, she is doing very well, and that is all I can tell you."

Curt just stared at him; he told me later that it scared him to death. Mr. D. could see the anxiety on his face and the surprise, but he did a great job of calming Curt down and sending him on his way. Before he left he suggested that Curt find some support for himself and not to try and go through this alone. He gave him a schedule of al-anon meetings and open AA meetings.

I was hoping he would start taking care of himself and learn about this disease for himself. He needed to look at his own alcohol and drug use. No matter how you look at it, drug use is wrong, it doesn't matter how little you do. His alcohol use had to stop in the house or I was not going home to him. The most important thing for me was to stay sober no matter what. I was not a good person or a fit mother when I was using, it took over my life and made me powerless—I was ready to get my power back and no one was going to stop me.

I decided that if Curt continued to use in front of me, I would enter a halfway home, get a job and take my girls. That decision had been made with the encouragement of the counselors. I was learning how to do what was best for me. I had not made choices for myself or made a decision in so many years that I was so afraid I would make the wrong ones. But I saw I was changing and when I talked I could hear my voice and that was so strange to me. I had a voice, I had something to say and I was proud of that.

I was appointed the floor monitor three weeks in a row; the first week I got it I started crying. I had to tell people what to do, and appoint jobs, make sure they were done and then check that they were done properly or speak to that person about doing it over. I was not popular.

It was completely new for me to be in a position where I directed people; hell I couldn't direct myself. I was a totally different person and it was starting to overwhelm me.

***

On the fourth week, while walking toward the counselor's station, I put my hands in my pockets and stopped dead in my tracks.

"What's the matter, Eileen?"

After a long pause, and me just staring ahead with a look of terror on my face, I pulled one of my hands out of my pocket, "there are pills in my jeans." I pulled out a small handful of familiar white pills.

"Yes we see that. Are those the jeans your husband brought you?"

"Yes, he planted these—I know he did. I don't understand, we cleaned the house from top to bottom; we got rid of everything. We even went through all my clothes, coats, purses, and went under everything, and on top, and down to the basement." I began to cry and the female counselor walked up to me, she was outspoken and got her point across quickly. Most of the patients were scared to death of her, but for some reason I wasn't. I knew I would get the straight up truth from her. We went to the meeting room alone.

"Give me the pills. Eileen, we both know where the pills came from. This isn't about you. Right now it's about your husband. When there is alcoholism in a family, it's not just the addict that is sick, but the whole family becomes sick and they take on their own roles, which you have been learning about. He is trying to sabotage your recovery because he is threatened by change. He needs you to need him; that's the way it's always been and he's afraid you're not going to need him anymore."

"In a lot of ways, I don't. I don't need him to buy my clothes, get the groceries, be the one to choose everything we have in the house, tell me when I can have money, how much, and what for. He made the decisions about everything: when we bought a car it was his decision, I never had any input. We need to have our furniture either replaced or reupholstered from the damage I have done; the girls need new to go school shopping and this is the first time I will demand to do it myself or do it together, but my input will be the major decision on what we get and I told him that."

"You need to be prepared when you get home because you will also get friction from your daughters. As much as they wanted you to stop using, they are going to have a hard time accepting the new you. You are probably the biggest personality transformation we have seen go through here after getting sober. So if it is apparent to us, imagine what your girls are going to feel. You have to be patient. They are going to be expecting Mom, but they are getting a new mom and it's possible they will push back and reject you.

"I have faith in you. You will do the right thing, we will give you many references for family counseling and individual counseling if you think the girls need it. This disease is cunning, baffling, and powerful—now I think you understand why that is such a strong statement."

I was starting to get angry. Curtis had been calling the counselors every night and telling them how to take care of me. The more I learned about the disease, the more I understood the powerful hold it had on both of us. It was up to me to remain strong and refrain from taking that first drink or drug! After everything that had happened, I still missed it. How sick is that? For me it is still very scary after all these years.

After discussing the pill issue with my primary (whom I had immense respect for), I agreed to see Curt. I knew I had a lot to say to him, but I was worried that I wouldn't go through with it.

Sunday came quickly for me. At one o'clock everyone's families started arriving. The counselor with the strong personality assured me that she would be there for me. Everyone's eyes were on me when he walked in. I was trembling, but when I saw him I stood up straight and remembered everything I had to say.

He had a small book in his hands. He walked right up to me and put his arms around me. I froze.

"Look what I have, it's the Al-anon book. I have been going to those meetings so I can support what is happening with you."

My eyes widened like huge saucers. "Well buster you are going to the wrong meetings, you need to be going to the same ones I am—AA. You know damn well you abuse drugs and alcohol. Who do you think you are kidding? Yourself? You probably have yourself convinced you are doing this wonderful thing, but cut the shit," the counselor came right up next to me and I could feel her body language saying *right on girl!*

"I will not come home to that house if you are still smoking pot or drinking. What do you think our girls are, stupid? They are smarter than we are and they know what you do too and they know about your affairs. We have been horrible parents and I mean WE. You have got a lot to learn about the disease of addiction or you will never learn how to be in this relationship. I will go to a halfway house, get a job, and get the girls so they can grow up in an alcohol- and drug-free home. The most important thing to me right now is staying sober. I want you to know that right from the start."

"You have become so selfish," he answered. "All you are concerned about is yourself. What about what you have put us through?"

I went crazy with anger. I could have punched him. Then I got it together because the last thing I wanted to do was lose it with him. I knew that I needed to put all of that in the past. I wanted to work on everything, but I had to slow down and take one thing at a time and now this was about sobriety.

He had stood there and listened to everything I said and I knew he was upset. He was not going to let anyone there know that. He looked straight into my eyes: "You are being brainwashed, I have never heard you talk to me this way. You are the selfish one—all you care about is sobriety. I don't believe it."

"Well you better, but it doesn't matter to me if you do or you don't. I know what I am going to do."

"Listen to yourself."

"I hear every word I am saying and I, for once, am sincere. I am scared too, but I am sincere and now you have your choices to make. You can be angry and think only of yourself and continue the way you have been, or you can quit using alcohol or any kind of drug if you want to try and make some kind of effort to rebuild our family. But you have to be substance free, Curt, and I mean it, or I am out the door.

"Our kids will never be subjected to that again. The deceit and manipulation is over for both of us. I know there is a lot I have done that you will never forget about, but there is also a lot you have done. You saw how sick I was in detox and how much pain I was in. I would have rather died and what did you do the first time we were alone on the way to rehab? You lit up a joint! How sick is that? I know I did as many or more sick things, so all of it has to be in the past, and if we are going to start over then we are going to start fresh. I want you to go talk with a counselor," and I pointed for him to go.

The counselor was right there and she let him have it too. "You are a sick man. We have a lot of work to do. You seem to know a lot about denial, but I would like to teach you some important facts." She was leading him toward the conference room as she spoke. "I want you to watch an educational video and learn something about this disease and understand what Eileen is trying to tell you...."

I could still hear their conversation and turned around just as she was telling him he was not helping himself or me by calling the floor every night and giving everyone directions on how to take care of me. "The only person you need to concentrate on taking care of is yourself. Eileen has done a great job learning to take responsibility for herself and now I am going to direct you in the same way."

I was so glad to see him go into the conference room with her. That was the first time I ever saw my husband do something he didn't want to do. I joined the rest of the group as if nothing had happened.

Admission

I had begun working on my fourth step, which was writing down every thing I had ever done to hurt or lie or manipulate anyone else. It was hard to go back twenty-five years when half the time had been spent in a black out, but I knew the people I had wronged.

The most humiliating experience of all was admitting all my wrongs to a person. Many patients chose loved ones or people they were close to, but I chose to speak to a priest. I met with a priest I didn't know; everything I told him stayed with him. I was embarrassed, ashamed, humiliated, and so painfully sorry for all the horrible things I had done. I admitted to stealing money and drugs, lying, and the worst admission of all was what I had done to my girls—I had brought them into this world practically fighting for their lives. There were so many things to admit to, but especially the pain I had caused others—it still hurts to talk about it today. I was a mess doing my fourth and fifth steps.

I spoke with Curt a few days after and he was very emotional. His day with the counselor was not a happy time, but it marked a very big change in his life. He learned a lot about himself and the disease and what was in his future. He had to face the fact that if he didn't get straight, I would not be going home.

He was confused about his feelings toward me. Neither of us felt love for one another. It was hard to admit to ourselves, but we had been married to each other for fifteen years and had never really loved each other; we were an addiction for each other.

He went to AA and got a sponsor. He then called our family doctor and got medical support so he could quit pot, he had been smoking since his early teens and had become mentally addicted.

I asked him to bring the girls up the next weekend. I was so nervous, it had been a long time since I had seen them and it had been hard for me. I was so happy when I saw them I couldn't stop hugging and kissing them and as angry as they were with me, they kept saying how different I looked and acted. Every time they said it they would start crying and I would start crying because I knew how they were happy about the change, but I could see the confusion in their faces. They weren't sure it would last.

"Mom, I've never known you like this, you're smiling and you look alive or something." All I could answer in return was how sorry I was. We didn't talk about anything in particular that day. They were in shock; that much was apparent. They hadn't expected to see what they saw. Now they were confused more than ever. They didn't stay long so we held hands and smiled at each other.

As they were leaving Missy looked at Curt and I and said: "Well this is weird, Dad is more and more like a different person every day and then we see you for the first time in so long and I can't stop looking at you."

Sara just kept holding my hand and smiling, it had always been her role to make sure everyone was happy and she finally got it—she was beaming. They left and I cried the rest of the night. The counselors came to talk to me a few times; they knew that day was incredibly hard for me. I asked every one of them "Have I changed a lot since I've been here?" They all reacted the same way; they laughed at first and said: "you better believe it."

Life was changing so fast for me and I didn't know where it was going. Would Curt and I end up together? Would things get better for the girls and me? What would I do with the rest of my life? My head was spinning. I had to keep reminding myself to take it fifteen minutes at a time. That was all I could handle at once.

The next few weeks were difficult to say the least. I was dealing with life and feelings without drugs or alcohol. I could not look at what was ahead or I would start to panic. I met with the counselors many times before my discharge and they were like different people from when I had arrived on that first day. They were encouraging and told me how proud they were of me. No one had ever said that to me before, so I would cry every time I heard it.

"Am I ever going to stop crying?"

"No, but that's okay. We straight people cry all the time."

I had said that it was the counselors who had changed from the first day I had arrived, but really it was me who had changed.

CHAPTER FIVE

Living Sober

It was time for me to go home and I finally understood why people were so hesitant to leave rehab. I was leaving my safety and security to deal with the world on my own and make my own decisions, I was trading structure for who knows what.

I was to attend meetings three times a day for thirty days. I thought of the planning and that I would have to find a babysitter for the girls, or maybe having to take them with me, or… thinking about it made me panic.

My counselor told me to stop projecting and just take "one day at a time" or in my case, fifteen minutes at a time.

The staff had written up a contract for Curt and I to sign. It stated that we would have no emotional or physical ties for one year. We needed to concentrate on our sobriety and our family as a unit and begin to heal first. I had no problem signing the contract. I didn't even know how I felt about Curt at that point. I knew I had become a different person, and if he was actually sober, he was different too.

Fifteen years of marriage and neither of us knew how we felt. We both agreed our priority was to stay sober and fix our family; from there we were walking into the unknown. The unknown meant change, and change scared the hell out of me. But I had conquered detox so I was on a roll. *Why stop now?* I was taking another risk, but it was different somehow. I had some confidence in myself and adopted the motto: "If it doesn't kill me, it can only teach me." So I went with that and tried not to look back.

I probably got fifteen minutes of sleep the night before I went home from rehab. I was so excited to see the girls and hold them and really feel them for the first time—ever. There were so many feelings and thoughts going on inside of me. I was excited to begin a life; until then I had just existed. It had been such an effort just to live day to day. That was about to change.

Since I was a little girl I can remember putting on an act for people and pretending to have some kind of personality. My life had been an act before rehab. I just took up space, space that someone who was productive and wanted to make something of life could have used. I had always felt like I needed to get out of the way. I know it sounds strange, but that is how I felt. I was in the way and when anyone saw me coming I imagined that they would think "oh no, here comes Eileen."

I felt as if I annoyed everyone and it didn't take long before people, even family, would become intolerant of me. Then I discovered alcohol and drugs, which I thought were my saving grace—my thinking was so twisted. Alcohol and drugs made me feel numb. I felt nothing for twenty-five years—absolutely nothing. I lived one day... and the next... and the next; I never had any plans or goals, but I would lie to my father and my family all the time. I would tell small lies, things not even worth lying about; and then there were the big ones. I was always about to get this great job or do something important. I would say anything I thought they wanted to hear; but then I would get back to self-medicating and feel nothing, which was the way I liked it. I didn't want to feel anything. If I could feel, I was in pain.

My life had spun out of control. My body was deteriorating and too many doctors had told me I was dying. Strangely enough I didn't want to live, but I didn't want to die either. That was the part of the disease that baffled me. I didn't like myself at all, but then there was that piece in my head that kept telling me I was the center of the universe. Everything was about me. I was always a victim or at least I thought I was.

When I left rehab I wasn't healed, but I had been given a lot of tools to stay on the road to recovery and I was ready to fight like hell to stay sober. No longer was I numb. I could feel the fear, the anxiousness, and for the first time, the happiness. I was actually aware of the fact that I was smiling, and it wasn't an act—it was odd, but it was good.

In rehab I had been given the gift of gratitude. I was grateful for the life I found there, of the mother I found for my children. I was able to admit to myself and to everyone in rehab that I was an alcoholic and my life had become unmanageable. I had gone in half-dead with no conception of what lie ahead, all I knew was that I was lucky to be alive— there was no hope for me unless I sought treatment. Thank God it was there for me. Thank God AA was there for me. That is how I learned of rehab. For the first time in my life, I played by the rules. Physically I went through hell while all the drugs and alcohol were flushed out of my body. Only then was I ready to confront my shit and I had a lot of it.

The morning I was to leave I felt very confused. I told one of the counselors I didn't want to leave and I burst into tears.

"What if I can't do it? What if the girls reject me? What if Curt and I start fighting?"

"What if, what if, what if," he said. "You are projecting, Eileen. Your fear comes from within. Now you are a human who can feel, you can see things the way they are now. You need to have more confidence in yourself. You just took the biggest risk of your life coming here and now the rest is up to you. We've given you the tools you need. Go to meetings. Find a female sponsor you can relate to. Stick to your contract with Curt. Put your sobriety first. You have more than enough work to do. Look for the positive in each other and learn to respect one another and the rest will come."

I felt so much better after talking to him. I was ready to take the risk. Rehab was a safe place, but I couldn't stay there the rest of my life. I had to learn to live life on life's terms. I started telling myself: *I can do this and I want to do this*. I really think that if you tell yourself something enough times, then eventually you will start to believe it.

Saying goodbye to the people I had bonded with was hard. They knew everything about me. They had gone through something so important with me and I will never forget them. I cried as I said goodbye. I was also smiling and feeling happy. I couldn't believe it, I was a different person. I had a hard time recognizing myself. What was my family going to think? I felt confident enough in myself to actually carry on a conversation with someone. *This is going to be unbelievable.*

Curtis and the girls arrived to take me home. I saw the girls and we all ran to each other and hugged for what seemed like an eternity. Sara looked up at me and asked: "Mom, why are you crying?"

I said, "I'm okay, you'll probably see me do this a lot, but I'm not sad, it actually makes me feel better."

"Are you sure Mom? You never cry."

"Honey, crying is a good thing." I told her. "When you don't see me crying anymore, that's when you should worry."

"What?"

"Never mind, we have a lot to catch up on and I have a lot to tell you." Missy looked at me and said, "you're so different, you're smiling even though you're crying."

"Because now I can feel and you'll understand more and more as we all get to know each other again." She just kept staring at me with her little face and every time I looked at her I saw her bottom lip quivering. So I began to tell them on the way home about my meetings and Alcoholics Anonymous. They0 were pretty surprised when I told them I would be going to a meeting three times a day for thirty days.

"Why?"

"Well, I drank every day, which wasn't a good thing, so instead I am going to go to a meeting everyday." I told them there were open meetings, which meant anyone could attend and closed meetings for just the alcoholics. I told them that they could go with me to the open meetings and sit with me and listen. They both looked at each other and then at me. Sara said: "I don't think I want to."

"We don't have to decide now, we'll talk about it later," I assured them.

"Wait until you see the house, Mom. Dad got new covers for the furniture." I felt a sickness in my stomach from the knowledge that I had destroyed the old stuff with all the accidents I had. "He got new curtains and bed clothes for our bedrooms. Everything looks so nice."

Curtis looked at me. He already knew I would have liked to help pick things out. So we had already gotten that out of the way. He knew he didn't have to do everything anymore. I was now capable and wanted to be part of everything. I so wanted us to be a family. Maybe that would happen, maybe it wouldn't. We were starting all over again.

***

We immediately started counseling, one-on-one and as a family. And of course there were also the meetings. We had to learn how to talk to one another, which I felt very good about because I really had no idea since we had always been so dysfunctional. It was very difficult though; we all had our own issues. Missy carried a lot of anger and Sara just wanted to make sure everyone was happy. With me not causing problems all the time, drinking and taking pills, Sara acted like everything was fine. She was locked up tight as a drum. In counseling, she didn't want to talk because as she put it: "I don't have anything to talk about, Mom stopped drinking so everything is fine." I knew that she would eventually erupt in some way, shape, or form.

I had come home an entirely different person. I was ready to be their mother and take care of them, but this was the role Missy had played for so long. It made her very angry that all of a sudden things were going to change and she had no say in it. Missy had been taking care of her sister for years and she resented me suddenly deciding to take that responsibility away from her when it was convenient for me. Her anger came out when I would ask her to do something, no matter how nice I asked.

"You don't have a right to tell me what to do—we did just fine without you."

This was difficult for me to handle. I was working on my own issues and one of them was dealing with my anger. I worked with my counselor, whom I adored. She had been with me since we had moved to Corning and she watched and helped me through my transition. She was also very shocked I had made it as far as I had.

My anger came to its peak one afternoon when one of the girls spilled Gatorade all over the kitchen floor, on accident, both of the girls just looked at me. My first reaction was to start yelling and carrying on. I looked up to see their little faces filled with fear. I stopped, shut my eyes, and took a deep breath.

This wasn't what I wanted for them. For what seemed like hours, so many thoughts and images went rushing through my mind. I saw the image of my mother's angry face and I could hear her voice, it kept getting louder and louder until I opened my eyes. I saw the girls' faces still staring, waiting for me to explode.

A feeling of calm came over me and I said: "its only Gatorade, how important is it?"

They looked at me dumbfounded and immediately looked at each other. They both gave a half smile and Missy said: "Yeah, its only Gatorade and it was an accident."

I wanted to cry. How many times in the past had I tormented them because of little things like that? I felt terrible for them. I told them to "come here" and they reluctantly walked over to me. I grabbed them and held them and said: "Today is the beginning of me not getting so angry over silly things. I am going to think before I open my mouth. I hope every time ends up like this, but I can't promise it will. I am going to try my best, and know that when I do get angry it's not because of you two. I've had a lot of anger inside me for a long time, and I am going to work as hard as I can to keep it together." They both looked at me with tears in their eyes and sighed in relief.

"I'm so sorry I have put you two through this, and Missy, I want you to think about yourself and those resentments and feelings of anger that you have towards me.

The more you talk about it and learn how to deal with it, the happier you'll be. You don't want to end up the way I have.

"Sometimes I count to ten when I feel that angry feeling coming on and it helps me to calm down. You know that you can always talk to your dad and I anytime and if you're not comfortable, you can talk to the counselor, right?"

"Okay, Mom."

Those years after rehab were so powerful for us. I was happy. I was sober.

Many good things were happening for me on a daily basis, even little things that people wouldn't generally notice. People came into my life; wonderful people who saw things in me. Things I was capable of that I never knew and they encouraged me to take risks I would never have taken on my own. The next thing I knew, I had a job that led to an even better job, and eventually I was a family worker for our school district.

I was given the opportunity to work with people whom I respected and I learned something new every day. I can't tell you how many times I have stopped and thanked God for everything in my life. My job that I loved so much, my family that was slowly healing and the simple things like a roof over my head. Also I had many great people in my life whom I had met in and out of AA. AA was teaching me how to live, and I needed a lot of teaching. I felt like a teenager just blossoming into adulthood.

So many things happened in those years, both good and bad. I started to develop a relationship with my father and siblings that wasn't based on alcohol.

Part of my job was teaching drug and alcohol prevention in the schools. I developed a friendship with one of my bosses; Ruth was a unique person who taught me so much, not only professionally, but also personally. She became a true friend. She taught me how to be the best at my job. She taught me about perception and that our reality is our perception. I started to go back to school, but soon realized that I could learn more from Ruth and our school social worker than any book could teach me. Honesty played and continues to play a big part in my sober life. So I tend to gravitate towards honest, upfront people. That was definitely Ruth, what you see is what you get with her and I admired that. How fortunate I felt to have someone like her in my life, especially at that time.

I looked forward to going to work every day; I truly loved my job. I also had supervision by the school social worker, Cheryl. She was the wife of the man in charge of the rehab I attended. He had been the one who continuously assigned me the job of floor monitor during my time in rehab. At the time it had scared the hell out of me, but he obviously knew what he was doing because it had helped me begin to develop self-confidence.

Gratitude

God had a reason for letting me live when I medically should have been dead and I was told that a million times. I don't believe in coincidence, I feel everything happens for a reason. God had surrounded me with wonderful people— they were a gift given to me. That is when I really started to learn about gratitude. Yes, I was grateful. I was grateful I was alive and had found AA and sobriety. But it became much more than that, I was living life with a purpose. I wasn't just wasting space anymore.

When the sincere feeling of gratitude for the simple things in life, a roof over my head and food on the table, hit me, it was a true spiritual awakening for me. I learned how to really pray. I became humble and got on my knees thanking God for my life and all the people in it. The more I let God into my life and believed everything that was happening for us was God's work, the more I realized it wasn't about me, but it was about what God wanted for me. He was in control, not me.

When these changes happened I began to feel the desire to stay sober for me, and not just my daughters. I WANTED to go to meetings—I looked forward to them. I started breaking the walls down around me and letting people into my life. I learned that we have so much to learn and gain from each other because each and every one of us has something to offer.

To this day, my mind is open to what people have to offer. I was also very fortunate to work with a woman who became a close friend of mine. She taught me about spirituality versus religion and the difference between them. Spirituality is something inside of me, a true honest feeling that continues to grow and help me to be a better person. This woman, Karen, was born with a gift. By watching her live and understanding her beliefs and how she practices them in everyday living, I came to understand that God was working through her. She gave so much to me. I never would have been able to experience that while I was drinking. I wouldn't have had all the wonderful relationships and experiences I've had in the last nineteen years if I was still using.

I didn't get sober and become a saint. I have many character defects, but the difference is that today I recognize them, accept them, and work at trying to improve them. Taking responsibility for my actions and being honest were the two most important things I learned early on. I struggled at first, everything was black and white for me, there was no gray area in my life, which drove my husband and other people in my life a little crazy.

I wanted to save the world from alcoholism and I felt it was my duty. I felt I had to give paybacks for the gift I had been given. With family and friends who I thought had a drinking problem, I tried to show them the way to sobriety. I was so brutally honest with people that at times it was a disadvantage to me. I was so overwhelmed with the changes in my life and the feeling of actually feeling happy that I wanted everyone to experience it.

However, the reality is that many people are not always interested in hearing the truth and now I realize that they are entitled to that. I was so amazed with the person I had become and I wanted to share it with the people I thought were in pain, to let them know they too can be happy. It took me a while, not to mention many people putting me in my place, before I finally realized that it was not my job to change the world.

I could only take care of myself and "lead" by example. The message I did continue to send was that know matter how low you think you are, there is still hope. I was scraping the bottom of the barrel and managed to pull myself out, so if I could do it, anyone can. There are so many resources out there and if you can just allow them in, you can find happiness.

For the survival of my family and my life, there were sacrifices I had to make in my social life. I didn't go to bars, attend parties where alcohol was being served, or hang out with people I used to drink with. Holidays had to be celebrated differently.

There were people I needed to make amends to. Some of those people didn't want to hear it because they had heard it all before. There were people who didn't want their children playing with mine; that broke my heart. Even though I was changing, once again because of my poor choices, my children had to suffer.

As a family, we started new traditions and had to learn all over again how to be a family. We are still working on that today. There is so much love between the four of us that we have ignored boundaries and that has caused some problems, especially as the girls got older. There were times in our girls' lives when Curt and I didn't belong, and there were places in our marriage that the girls didn't belong. But we were all so intertwined with each other, and somewhat confused as to exactly what our role was in the family, that we constantly pissed each other off. When the girls became adults, we were once again alone, trying to find our place in life besides being parents. The girls had separation issues when they went away to college.

My famous sober statement was: "There is so much in a day I want to do, it seems like a waste of time to have to sleep." I said this often because I was enjoying my life, my family, and my job. We were not and are not anywhere near being wealthy or rich people, but we both worked very hard and had the necessities we needed in life. For me that was so awesome after growing up in a family of ten and very little money.

I remember the first time I went and bought groceries for the week, something I didn't do in my addiction, and I was able to get all of the things we needed and a few extras. I always bought the bargains, but I remember coming out of the grocery store with my cart full of groceries and I started crying because it felt so good to be able to get my family the things they needed. I felt like a child just experiencing life for the first time and in many ways I was.

When I was able to take the girls clothes shopping the first time, I had the same reaction, but this time they were with me and I grabbed hold of them just hugging them and telling them how wonderful it was to be able to do this for them. They looked at me like I had two heads; it was like I stepped into a world I knew nothing about.

In AA they call how I felt during those first years of sobriety being on a pink cloud, but in many ways that pink cloud has never left. It was unbelievable how much and how fast my life continued to change in sobriety. I was developing relationships, I had a fantastic job that I was good at, and my family was learning to respect one another.

Control

While I was in my addiction, I was consumed with how I would get my next drink and drug. I became a master manipulator when it came to getting my various prescriptions from different doctors, so when I entered recovery, I worked just as hard to be the best recovering addict—in doing so, I was still trying to control things.

The first thing I learned in AA was that while I was in my addiction, I was the one in control. I couldn't see how many good things I had in my life because I put drugs and alcohol first, but that all came crashing down. The people I love didn't want anything to do with me and I hated myself. I didn't care that I was killing myself. And so I also learned my first mistake when I was in recovery: Trying to remain in control when it was out of my control.

When I was in control, my life was a disaster. Soon I discovered that all I had to do was let go and listen. I was spiritually bankrupt when I got sober. When I really got honest with myself I started to experience a spiritual awakening—letting go was my first experience and it felt so powerful.

I've heard many people say they lost the desire to use in AA. Not me. I never lost the desire to hide behind a fog when I started to experience negative feelings, but that was no longer an option for me. That became a problem when I had to take medications after surgeries and during some health problems. I have had to learn to deal with that part of my life; it is a constant battle.

***

One relationship I missed during my years in addiction was with my little sister; she is a year younger than I. After I started using, our relationship became strained, she couldn't watch me destroy myself. I believe she was hesitant when I first got out of treatment, but the longer I stayed sober, the closer we got. I began to realize how much I had missed the closeness we shared growing up together. We don't live close to each other now, but when we do see each other it's always good.

Recovery made it possible for me to care about other people, it allowed me to get outside myself and see a whole new wonderful world I had missed for so many years. I also began to see that I wanted to make a difference—for the first time, I genuinely cared.

So many good things happened to me when I stopped using, I was able to support my girls in their goals—they both ended up receiving athletic scholarships to college. I got a job helping and empowering people.

Slowly but surely I was making connections to different people and breaking down the protective walls I had worked so hard to build during my addiction. It was nice to let people in. I was developing sincere relationships built on trust and caring. I saw my girls watch these changes in me and it was wonderful to witness them take similar risks and let those protective walls lower bit by bit.

I am in awe of the way my daughters have coped with their pain and the choices they have made to get through it. I thank God that Missy and Sara did not choose the path I chose. I used alcohol and drugs to cope with my pain and continued to use until I was so physically and mentally addicted that I felt trapped in a world with no doors. Then I experienced a miracle.

I found a very small door, but I had to reach out to a lot of people to get me through that door. Many people reached out and showed me the right direction to take—for them I am eternally grateful.

Living With Alzheimer's

At 55 years old I have Alzheimer's disease, but I continue to surprise myself every day. In my addiction I had no drive, I had no desire, but being sober has brought me days where I truly believe I can do anything. I used to tell my husband (before I got sick), "sleep is such a waste of time, those are hours and minutes I could be up and enjoying all these great things life has to give."

It sounds corny as all hell and when I would say it I would burst out laughing at myself, but I believed it. There weren't enough hours in the day for me to do all the things I wanted to do in my job, with my family—in all aspects of my life.

I continued working for the school district until 2003 when my health declined and I was told I could no longer work. Most of it was a consequence of my addiction. I was very sad to quit working, I loved my job—it had become my identity and I loved the people I worked with.

After I retired I started having problems and was placed on various medications, which I stopped fighting with my doctor about. I know I was looking for something to make me feel better, my recovery was in jeopardy and I made a few mistakes because I let my guard down and I wasn't going to many meetings. I found out then that AA was one of the major keys to keeping me sober.

The past four years, since I've been diagnosed, have brought a fog back into my life that is reminiscent of my addiction years. It started out as forgetfulness and then moved into feelings of disorientation during familiar activities or tasks. I began finding myself in places suddenly, not knowing why I was there. I began having difficulty recognizing familiar people in my life whom I've known for years.

Since my mental state has begun to worsen, I've once again witnessed pain and fear in the eyes of my girls. They have been helping my husband fight through the denial of this diagnosis. Curtis and I have been married for 32 years. During this past year he has been the most supportive, loving, and loyal husband to me.

There are days when I cannot even get out of bed and I don't know why. I've lost my independence, which was very important to me. I cannot drive or do many things alone; however that stubborn streak in me comes back when I am having a good day and I feel like no one can hold me back, yet in a flash I feel weak, insecure, and scared. I don't even ask why anymore because I know why; taking drugs, over one hundred pills on some days and drinking alcohol everyday for twenty-five years. I truly believe, as well as my doctors, that this abuse has contributed to the early onset of Alzheimer's.

I cry a lot now. I don't want things to end now for me. I want more grandchildren; I want more years of love with my family. Things are moving too fast, but I'm going to a great

Alzheimer's research clinic and if there is hope for me, it will come. We just keep praying because I feel like I have a lot of life left in me. At times, I'm just a bit goofy is all. That is how I see best to describe myself, especially at this stage of the disease. Everyone is different and symptoms vary.

I pray that I'm able to have many more wonderful years with my family and friends. I have had the opportunity to work for and meet great friends in my life. They are supportive and I believe I have said before, its hard for me to believe I am worthy of having such caring people in my life after the pain I have caused so many people over the course of my life. But I work every day to pray for the courage to forgive myself.

One thing I have learned about myself is that I really am a good person and it's easier for me to forgive others, be non-judgmental of other people, and be there whenever I am needed for someone else. My goal for today is to be as kind to myself as I am to other people.

***

My husband and I cry together, afraid of the unknown, but also knowing that God has a plan for me. Part of that plan, I believe, is to write this book and share with the world the plain fact that if this can happen to me, it can happen to anyone. If this book touches just one person's heart and mind and helps them in some way, then I have achieved what I set out to do.

That pit in my stomach rushes back every time I know of or think about other people suffering from addiction of any kind. It gets a hold of you and manipulates you, toys with you until it has you hooked. My heart goes out to anyone experiencing this.

My family and I have discussed the repercussions of writing this book and being so brutally honest about what has happened in our lives. People are judgmental and they will judge me and that's okay. But if you are judging me, dig deep down inside yourself to see if you can relate to anything you have read in this book, whether it's for you or someone you know. Know that there is a doorway that leads to a better life—there is help out there. AA was and is my savior, but there are other ways as well. Find what it is that works for you and don't be afraid of it; just dive in with everything you've got.

Epilogue

Letters From My Girls

A Letter From Missy

Many of my childhood memories are vague—almost like a story you can't quite remember the details to, but you know how it turns out. However, there are a handful of memories I can remember like they happened yesterday. I'm not exactly sure why I remember what I do or what it is about those specific times, but I'm sure they are significant.

Unfortunately, most of what I remember is neither good nor negative, which is probably connected to why I sometimes consider myself to be an angry person. But thanks to my son and finally being in a happy and healthy relationship, I think my anger has subsided significantly. I am finally at a point in my life where I think I understand what is actually important.

And now, as our family is experiencing the Alzheimer's rollercoaster, I feel like I grow up a little more each day and appreciate what I once took for granted.

My earliest memory is of when I was quite small. I don't think I could have been much older than four years old. I remember wearing a little pink dress and being in the living room of a guy my parents bought drugs from. My dad was on the couch, the guy was in a chair and mom was drunk in the kitchen. I remember just walking around the house, being deathly afraid of a dog they had, which we called "Cujo" because he was so scary, watching my parents drink and smoke pot. Even as a little kid I knew it was all wrong so I tried anything to get their attention, because if they were yelling at me, they weren't drinking or smoking. And if I kept it up enough, they would get pissed off and we would leave.

108

My feelings early on were mostly of worry. Feeling worried that they were going to die, because that's what the commercials said; feeling worried that the police would find out and take them to jail; feeling worried that our neighbors and my friends would find out. The latter worrying started when I became old enough, seven or eight, to go play at friends' houses—always friends in the neighborhood so I could walk home at any time to make sure mom was ok.

Dad usually wasn't home, but I felt like he was stronger than Mom and I didn't really need to keep an eye on him. I really didn't have much of a relationship with my dad until I started playing sports. He worked and did what he did and it was usually mom, Sara and I. The worrying consumed me and when I couldn't take worrying anymore, it turned to anger.

I equally loved and hated my mother from the time I was eight years old. It wasn't until the end of college that I finally allowed myself to understand the disease of alcoholism and addiction—then my hatred started to subside.

When we moved to Corning, our family befriended another family in the neighborhood. I made friends with the oldest daughter. Our mothers also became friends and we often did things together. It was then that I realized my mom was not like most others. This made me angry and jealous. I wanted to be my friend and I wanted her to be me. I remember so often feeling like I was inadequate and my mom is the way she is because of me. So whenever my friend and I would have a snack, play a game, or do anything that required a choice to be made, I would think about what I wanted and be sure not to choose it. Maybe if I chose what my friend wanted, I would be different; more like her and my mom would be more like her mom. Of course, it never happened, but as a child it made sense.

When Mom hit rock bottom and had to go into rehab, things changed. The worrying stopped, no more hiding drugs, bongs or shit-smelling couch cushions. I entered a whole new world of dysfunction. I was filled with anger, resentment and confusion.

I can remember a few days after Mom came home from rehab, I was playing outside with Sara, it was getting dark and Mom was up the street at an AA meeting. She had come home and said it was time to come in. I had feelings of rage, "who the hell was she telling me what to do?" She hadn't acted like a mom up until then and suddenly she was ready and I was supposed to just go along with it? It made me so angry.

She was suddenly the one who got to decide what was going to happen because she decided to stop abusing pills, doing drugs and getting drunk. It was a huge adjustment going from taking care of Mom and Sara, to being taken care of. I had no idea how to do it.

I was ten when she got sober and spent the rest of my childhood feeling like my parents owed me. They could never do enough. Even when I wasn't angry, I was mad. As I got older, I denied the anger and tried to convince myself I was over it. Deep down I knew I wasn't because every time I would be in a conversation where I mentioned my parents were recovering alcoholics, my lip would quiver and my face would burn up. I never really could talk about it without getting upset until probably a couple years after I graduated college. Up until that time I still had this deep down feeling that I was the only one in the world who had alcoholic parents and I still needed to hide it. Now I realize that there are many people out there with alcoholic/drug addict parents, some in recovery and, may God bless them, some who aren't.

I'm not sure of exactly the time when I finally allowed myself to understand the concept of alcoholism and it being a disease. It began to happen while I was in college because that was when I decided to have my first drink. I had been so against drinking, I hated it. I even hated people who did it. But a couple months into my freshman year of college, I decided to try it. I loved it.

That first year I drank a lot, so much that I almost left school because I wanted to have fun more than work hard at basketball. I was going to transfer to a Division III school where I would have more freedom. Luckily, I didn't and I opened my eyes. I became fearful that I would end up like my parents. So I finally started internalizing everything I had been told about alcoholism, that it can be inherited and it is a disease. I didn't stop drinking, but I controlled it.

I finally understood that alcoholism is a disease, and for one reason or another, it can suck a person in. And once it's got you, it never lets go. It's up to the person to choose to fight it, or let it take over.

My mom didn't abuse pills and get drunk everyday because I was a bad daughter, she didn't do those awful things because she loved them more than me, which was what I thought was the case. This thinking was what drove most of my anger. She did them because she is an addict. To be plagued by addiction is a horrible thing and I thank God I didn't inherit that trait. It's probably a miracle that I didn't, given that both of my parents battle it everyday of their lives. But regardless of what they've done wrong, because they love us so much, they had the strength to make the most important decision of their lives, as well as mine, which was to stop abusing drugs and alcohol and get sober. For that, I am ever so grateful. Because of their decision, I was given the chance to make better choices and live a successful life.

A Letter From Sara

What's wrong with my mom? Why doesn't she act like everyone else's mom? I was six years old when I first realized my mom was different from everyone else's; one afternoon she drove a car full of my friends and I all over town in search of Pop Rocks® candy. My friends thought she was so cool because their parents didn't even want them to eat Pop Rocks®, but not my mom. She was obsessed; we drove for more than hour until we finally found some.

When one of my friends told her mom what we had been doing I could tell she thought it was strange from her reaction. But no matter what she did, I always loved her and

NEVER wanted to make her mad. If my mom was angry or upset I knew it was my job to fix it and if I didn't, then I figured it was my fault that she was mad in the first place.

I was four years old when we moved to Painted Post, NY and when we first pulled up, I saw a little girl my age. She came right over and we became best friends from the start. We played together every day either at my house or at hers, but I couldn't figure out why it was so different at her house. I would watch how her mom was and I wished that my mom would be like that, but I knew deep down it wouldn't happen.

As time passed I made more friends, but I stayed home when Mom "wasn't feeling well," so I could take care of her. My real issues started when I had to go to school. I felt that I couldn't leave my mom home alone all day. Who would take care of her? I didn't want to play with my friends as much because I didn't want to leave Mom home alone. I learned to adjust after awhile and I tried to be like the other kids as much as possible.

Sports became my coping mechanism. My sister and I played anything and everything we could. Mom and Dad finally let me join a tee-ball team since I loved to play so much. This meant that my mom would be coming to my games and talking to the other parents; I was nervous because I knew they would see her drunk. This was about the time I started finding empty bottles of beer and drugs left out from the night before.

My sister and I would get up early so we could put everything back in order so Mom and Dad wouldn't get into a fight. As time continued this was becoming an everyday event.

We were starting to figure out what the drugs were and thought that if we threw them out then maybe Mom wouldn't use them, but that wasn't the case. All that did was create more fights, more drinking, and more taking care of Mom. As she continued to worsen, I began full days in school, but I was so overwhelmed with the fear that my mom needed me that I would go home sick at least once a week. Once I got home I felt much better; I was always able to convince myself that I couldn't have possibly stayed in school or something bad would have happened.

I clearly remember coming home from school one day and finding my mom in the backyard passed out. She had leaves all over her and it looked like she had fallen out of the second story window. When she got up I knew that she was on something and had really fallen, all that did was make me worry even more about her.

Times continued to worsen; the last time I had to deal with my mom being drunk and on drugs was the night she and I were home alone. I was eight years old. She was making me dinner while I sat on the couch watching television. All of the sudden I heard a loud bang that sent a shudder through the house. I ran to the kitchen. She was sprawled out on the kitchen floor with her head banging violently against the freezer.

When the ambulance arrived they told me mom would be going away for a while—"say goodbye," they had said. I felt horrible because I had asked her to make me food, which in my mind caused her accident. I thought it was my fault.

I couldn't shake that horrible feeling of guilt for a long time.

Soon after Mom went into detox and then rehab; she was gone for a few months and Dad was really struggling to take care of my sister and me.

We finally made it through mom being gone; it was time to go pick her up. We were so excited. We did everything we could to make the house look good and to be on our best behavior. Dad had the furniture re-upholstered, house cleaned and painted, laundry done; we knew she was going to be so happy.

It was kind of weird seeing Mom for the first time; I didn't really know how to act. I was so excited to see her, but how was it going to be with her not drinking? It took some adjustment. I could tell Missy was angry with her, but I was happy that she was home. I spent every moment I could with her and I hated to leave her alone. Dad worked nights so Mom drove us to practice and everyplace we wanted to go.

She explained to us what it meant to her to not drink and to go to her meetings every night. All I wanted was for her to be happy. If she had to go a few times a day that was ok with me, I loved her so much and I just wanted to be able to make it all better.

I was about ten years old when my friends convinced me to stay the night for the first time. I agreed, but I was scared to leave Mom. I was convinced that she needed me at home. I made it a few hours before I got "sick" and called her to come pick me up. I did this for a few years; I don't think I was capable of staying at someone else's house without my mom until I was about 13 years old.

I knew that this was not normal, but I didn't know how to get over it. My daily priority was to make Mom happy at all costs and I would get so mad at Missy for being angry and not treating Mom well. Missy still tried to take charge because she had done it for so long. She had one role and I had another, but neither of us mentioned our feelings.

As time continued I began to deal with my issues—mom could survive without me. She would apologize to me for drinking and doing drugs when she was pregnant with me, but I always said, "Mom its ok, I love you so much and I don't even think about it."

That was the truth, because I didn't want her to be sad or beat herself up about it because it wouldn't change the past anyway. High school years went by relatively smoothly, we were all learning how to deal with our issues, but Missy was still angry.

I was always happy and never wanted to talk about anything. Mom tried to make us go to a counselor numerous times but I hated going, I hated talking about it because it brought up unhappy memories. I understood alcoholism was a disease; it wasn't her fault so why did we need to talk about it? I never really had any major breakdowns from our childhood, I just held it all in.

I had never drank before college because I couldn't do that to my mom, I saw what she had done to us and I could never insult her by drinking. Well, things change when you are away from home and Mom and Dad aren't around all the time. I began to experience college, I went out and had fun, but I still had to check in on my mom every day, usually three or four times a day. It was my way of making sure that she was doing okay.

My first year in college went by relatively smoothly, but as the year continued I developed an eating disorder. I did everything I could to hide it; I think it was my own form of control, my way of dealing with not being there for my mom everyday. It was the only thing I had control over, and I was going to do it well. I made it through a year without letting anyone know, but my family knew without me telling them. For so long I had said that I was fine, "I don't need to talk about things," but it all backfired on me.

I have suffered from anorexia and bulimia for the past eight years—it was all part of my coping mechanism.

I look back on my childhood and wish that it could have been more normal, but I have accepted that I can't change it. My mom has suffered enough and I do not hold any resentment toward her. We are a close family that is there for each other any time of the day or night. I am thankful that in spite of everything we are happy and we love each other unconditionally.

Hard Look at Addiction

A Letter From My Pharmacist

A man called the pharmacy several times one morning to see if his doctor had called in a prescription, Ultram (tramadol). The man had shown a pattern of overuse in recent weeks. The drug is not a controlled substance, but is a habit-forming pain reliever. When I took the doctor's call, I recognized the voice as being that of the patient, not the doctor. Luckily, I knew the physician well enough to call his office and ask if they had just called in the prescription. They had not. I told the physician what the patient had done and that I would be calling the local police. The physician was concerned that the patient would experience dangerous withdrawal symptoms.

I phoned the police, and they suggested that we set it up so they could be in the store when the patient came in. I did. The police were waiting when the man arrived. He continued to deny any wrongdoing as they handcuffed him and took him away.

The physician called back a short time later and explained that a short investigation revealed that the patient had gotten many samples from their office. They also discovered that he had successfully called in several more orders for the drug at other pharmacies in town. They estimated that he had obtained over five hundred tablets in less than two weeks. The doctor reiterated his concern about withdrawal—anyone taking that much medication would certainly crash quickly if they abruptly stopped. I called the police to express that concern.

Two weeks went by and the man's name appeared in the local obituary column. He had been dead for three days before they found him in his apartment—he was surrounded by dozens of empty tramadol bottles.

My emotions were mixed when I found out that he had died. At the time of his arrest, I was angry to think that someone would so boldly try to manipulate the system. Then when he died, I felt guilty for feeling angry. I felt like he hadn't been given enough help after the arrest. Maybe there was something more I could have done.

I have worked as a pharmacist for twenty-six years in this community. This is my hometown, a town where the medical community is very small and close-knit. Most of the doctors know my voice or have heard about my good reputation from others.

However, a small town medical environment can be

cruel to prescription addicts who are trying to turn themselves around. Eventually the network of doctors and pharmacists will catch on and turn them away. Someone like Eileen who has been manipulating that network for years will find it difficult to get medical care after a while. She has had to find doctors and pharmacies willing to look past her history and give her credit for her efforts at recovery.

Professionals should try to remain unbiased, but it's difficult to believe a person who has lied and manipulated for so long. Addicts will go to great lengths to get their drugs. They will travel to surrounding towns. They will claim to have no insurance so their tracks will be more difficult to follow, otherwise all of their medical visits can be accessed electronically.

Many people have learned that I can be a real hard-nose if they lie to me. Just last week I had someone show up with prescriptions from an unsuspecting physician. I reported the customer. The police questioned him and turned him in to his parole officer. The doctor told me to shred the prescriptions. I later called the other pharmacies to warn them.

I could fill a whole book with such stories. They are all the same. Success stories are rare, but occasionally I hear of people who have turned their lives around. I admire those people. To overcome the small town whispers and stories can be as difficult as kicking the drug addiction itself.

I am a recovering alcoholic. My own recovery has kept me optimistic through the years. My addiction is not an everyday struggle, but it never goes away. An addict can never be recovered. But recovery can become easier over the years, especially if you remind yourself of your worst lies, the lies you told yourself for so many years.

Sadly, my profession has a high rate of alcoholism and drug addiction. Those of us dealing with our own addictions should be the most tolerant and the least hypocritical; and yet there are those who choose to pass judgment. Recovering addicts should be praised for their strength and courage.

I want to believe that anyone can beat addiction—if the desire is there. I'm overly critical of the ones who keep coming back with the same old stories and I am not afraid to tell them to stay away. They eventually catch on and stop coming in. Those who know me know that I will help anyone who is serious about recovery; I play by the rules, but I can be their best listener and supporter if they give me a chance.

Karen Hogue
Pharmacist, 26 years
Corning, NY

***

I thank Karen so much for her honesty and her loyalty. She has been my pharmacist for more than ten years and has been a godsend. She confronts me on my crap and calls my doctors if she thinks something will be a trigger. I believe she really cares about me and knows how important my recovery is to me. She listens when I am having a bad time and she lets me know when I am not being honest with myself. She has taken care of my family for years and is the best friend I could ever have and I hope she feels the same. There are not enough words Karen to tell you how much you have helped my family and me. -- Eileen

Appendix

The Facts of Addiction

Why Can't I Have Just One?

Alcohol is not always a bad thing. There are many people who will never struggle with alcoholism, they enjoy a glass of wine with dinner, or meet friends for a drink or two and enjoy good conversation. Not for me. I hate the fact that drinking for me is out of the question; there is no such thing as just one.

The first half of my life was a struggle to find the willpower to have just one, or even two. There are many people who will never understand the pain and solitude of addiction; those are the people who can stop at one drink and one piece of chocolate, they live in moderation—I am not one of those people.

Addiction comes in many forms: alcohol, drugs, food, relationships, sex, shopping—the list goes on. Alcohol is considered a drug because it is mind altering, just like narcotic prescription drugs, street drugs like cocaine, speed, heroine, mushrooms, crack and many more. For the person who suffers from addiction, it is simply not possible to have just one. An addict is powerless. The addiction controls our actions and our decisions; in short, an addict's life becomes unmanageable.

The American Council on Alcoholism (ACA) compares alcohol to a sandbox. Alcohol consumption enables individuals to stick their heads in the sand and avoid issues, problems, and most of all, *feelings*. But, the pain does not go away, it simply lurks until the alcoholic takes his or her head out of the sand, then the pain becomes unbearable and relapse is common. Addicts simply cannot deal with problems. The pain that addicts feel when they stop consuming alcohol or drugs is insurmountable—that is, without outside help.

The ACA says it's the emotional issues caused by an imbalance in the brain that causes relapse. Relapse is a part of the disease and commonly leads right back to the consequences that drinking causes. Social drinkers and people who do not drink at all cannot typically understand what makes alcohol-dependent people drink when they are very aware of the consequences caused by drinking. I know first-hand how true this is. I lost count of how many times I had promised to stop: *this time I am going to stop for good.* My family lost faith in my empty promises. They wanted desperately to believe me, to believe in me, but I had hurt them too many times with my lies and deceit.

I now understand the disease and the pain I had caused all of the people who loved me most.

Understanding the Female Addict

Much of what I learned about women and why they abuse substances is from the book *Women Under the Influence*. It explains that women are more likely to abuse than men. Women drink to lose weight, relieve stress or boredom, improve their moods, reduce sexual inhibitions, to self-medicate depression and pain or negative feelings they may be experiencing—which is the reason I started drinking.

Alcohol gives a false sense of self-confidence. Women in treatment are five times more likely to have been sexually molested as children and to suffer from eating disorders. A National Center on Addiction and Substance Abuse at Columbia University study revealed that women are more likely to start drinking heavily after a crisis such as a miscarriage, divorce, unemployment, or when a child leaves the home. Older women are more likely to self-medicate with alcohol and prescription drugs to deal with financial insecurity or loss of a spouse.

An alcoholic doesn't drink to feel good; they drink so they don't feel bad.

Statistics show that women who have never married, or are divorced or separated are more likely to drink heavily and experience alcohol-related problems. Unmarried women living with a partner are more likely to engage in heavy drinking and develop drinking problems.

Women who abuse alcohol or even drink to excess face greater risks to their health than males. Alcohol increases a woman's risk of heart disease, liver disease, ulcers, reproductive problems, osteoporosis, pancreatitis, memory loss and other serious illnesses. In the late stages of alcoholism, women also develop hypertension, anemia and malnutrition.

The American Medical Association discovered that a woman's risk of breast cancer rises with the amount of alcohol she regularly consumes. Menstrual disorders have also been associated with alcoholism. A pregnant woman risks the life of her unborn child because the alcohol in the blood is carried to the baby's bloodstream, which can lead to a miscarriage, fetal alcohol syndrome, fetal alcohol effects, and birth defects. My youngest daughter suffered from fetal alcohol effects.

Today I live with the pain and guilt that my daughter was an innocent victim of my destructive behaviors before she even breathed her first breath on this earth. The problems associated with drinking while pregnant are so great that women should stop drinking before trying to get pregnant.

In today's society, young women are drinking earlier in life and are fifteen times more likely than men to use illegal drugs by the age of fifteen. To make matters worse, treatment for women continues to lag behind because the female anatomy is more complex and also because women face a greater social stigma that hinders the desire to seek treatment.

Alcoholism Affects the Entire Family

Alcoholism affects more than the drinker, it affects the whole family. As the drinking increases, he or she ignores all other responsibilities and concentrates on getting the next fix. The needs of the household take a back seat to the addict as the entire family shifts their concern from their own needs to the needs of the alcoholic. This was the case in my house—it was a house, not a home and for me there is a difference. The focus was on my behaviors and me. My family worried about me all the time, my husband worried every time he walked out the door. I was controlling everyone. Sadly, I remember all too well what that was like for me as a child who feared my own mother.

Alcoholism brings its own chaos into the family system. There is no way to predict an alcoholic's behavior and compensate for it. Each member of the family adopts his or her own role. The most common roles are:

1. The Caretaker tends to everyone else's needs and in the process stops seeing to their own needs.
2. The Mascot/Cheerleader tries to provide levity (gaiety) to the family.
3. The Lost Child disappears from the activity of the family. Their favorite places are in front of the TV or shut away in their rooms. They tend to have issues with weight and are very low maintenance.
4. The Hero is always making things better. He or she is the one everyone depends on.
5. The Scapegoat is always getting negative attention, being blamed for the alcoholic drinking, has issues with authority figures.

These roles can change over the years to meet the dynamics of the family. In our family, my older daughter Missy took on the role of the caretaker. She was the mother in our family—she took care of her sister, got her ready for school, and fed her when I wasn't in any shape to make meals; she watched over Sara in and outside the home, she was there for her dad when he had to go to work. My daughter Sara was the cheerleader; she always wanted everyone to be happy.

Denial Enables the Addict and Just Plain Stops Recovery

One definition of denial is living with oneself while living a lie. Denial is also a defense mechanism to avoid responsibility by rejecting reality. Denial is resistance to change and the mind's attempt to rationalize painful realities that for the alcoholic are a way to avoid dealing with the fact that alcohol and drugs are destroying your life and your loved ones.

Denial is a major obstacle for both the alcoholic and the nonalcoholic. It had a huge impact on my family's life for many years. My husband, at some point in our life, started to drink as a means of coping with the problems my alcoholism had been causing in the family; but he stayed in denial about it for quite some time, which kept him from addressing his problem—not to mention mine. Ultimately denial kept me from getting treatment because I convinced myself that I could quit on my own anytime.

Denial is a form of enabling. While helping is doing something for someone that they are not capable of doing for themselves, enabling is doing for someone else what they could and should be doing for themselves.

In an alcoholic home, denial creates an atmosphere in which the alcoholic can comfortably continue his or her unacceptable behavior. Early in my life and into my teens and early twenties, my father was my enabler. I was often in financial trouble because I could not hold down a job. I was always in some kind of trouble. My father was always there to save me from whatever trouble my drinking would get me into. He loved me and thought he was helping me, but really he was enabling me by keeping me from suffering the consequences of my behavior.

When I married my husband, he became the enabler and then through example, my children later became enablers. My family kept my secrets safe in a feeble effort to keep me happy.

My husband did all the things an enabler does; he took on all the traits of a classic codependent. This is a pattern of behavior that we typically learn growing up. Codependency is a type of enabling because in an effort to fix the addict, it only worsens. The substance abuser creates more problems while the codependent tries not to rock the boat and controls the situation with manipulation.

There are ten things you must never do if you are in an alcoholic relationship.

1. Don't deny alcohol is causing problems in your family or relationships.
2. Don't deny the deep emotional problems that alcohol is having on your children or yourself.
3. Don't think that people are unaware or your situation.
4. Don't think things will change by themselves.
5. Don't try to control their drinking or think you can.
6. Don't make excuses or protect the alcoholic from the consequences of their behavior.
7. Don't give an ultimatum that you won't follow through on, say what you mean, mean what you say, or don't say it.
8. Don't allow yourself to be manipulated, controlled, or provoked verbally or by the actions of the alcoholic. Be proactive not reactive.
9. Don't let them make you feel responsible for their drinking or the problems caused by the drinking.
10. Don't believe the promises of an alcoholic until the test of time proves them to be true.

These are important points to know and follow. I wish I had had this information when I was a teenager—it might have made the difference in my life. They helped my daughters. Detachment from alcoholics doesn't mean you're abandoning them. After spending many years with this disease and after trying everything possible to keep the situation from getting worse, I know recovery is nearly impossible without the help of the people they are closest to. As a loved one, it is your job to focus on you and no longer:

1. Allow suffering because of the actions and reactions of others.
2. Allow yourself to be used or abused by others.
3. Do for others what they can do for themselves.
4. Manipulate situations so others will eat, sleep, get up, pay bills, and/or not drink.
5. Cover up for the mistakes of others.
6. Avoid a crisis situation or prevent it when it should the normal cause of events.

It is more difficult to stop enabling than it is to keep up with old habits. This can be a painful transition, but a necessary one. The following examples are typical behaviors of an enabler:

1. Calling in sick for the alcoholic.
2. Making excuses or lying for the alcoholic.
3. Performing some or all of the alcoholic's secular work duties.
4. Not discussing the drinking to avoid a fight.
5. Accepting part of the blame for the alcoholic's drinking or behavior.
6. Covering for the alcoholic when they are supposed to be somewhere or doing something.
7. Bailing the alcoholic out of jail and or paying legal fees.
8. Believing the lies of the alcoholic and then speaking on his or her behalf when he or she is accused of something improper or criminal.
9. Emotionally buying into the alcoholic's current crisis lock, stock and barrel and then reacting inappropriately.
10. Protecting the alcoholic from consequences of actions.

11. Buying weaker booze so you can control their drinking.
12. Giving in to their request of "one more drink."
13. Taking responsibility for chores, duties, finances and children's needs.
14. Taking sole responsibility for the income of the home.
15. Giving the alcoholic one chance after another.
16. Giving ultimatum's without following through.
17. Cleaning up messes and fixing mess-ups.
18. Taking numerous daily crisis phone calls from the alcoholic that interrupts you at work.
19. Drinking with them in the hopes of controlling they're drinking.
20. Paying their bills.
21. Not pressing charges after a domestic abuse fight.
22. Pretending things are fine to avoid a fight.
23. Agreeing to make-up sex after a fight they started.
24. Not going somewhere to avoid a fight.

If you want to help the alcoholic then you need to take care of yourself and make yourself happy first; you deserve it. Often when we stop being codependent and enabling the addict, it triggers a fear of loss in him or her and can drive people to seek help. This was true for me, it really scared me when my husband and children chose not to take care of me anymore—I hit bottom. I knew I had to get help or lose them forever.

All the Right Reasons

Every reason is the right reason to get help! I didn't get into treatment for me; I did it to save my family. It doesn't matter what the reason is, what's important is that the alcoholic gets help. There is a saying in the program: "keep coming until you do it for you," and that was how it happened for me.

My life got better quickly that first year. I was no longer using, my children were less angry, and we were working together as a family. One day on my way to a meeting, I found myself happy to be going and realized I was looking forward to it—finally, I was doing it for me.

Treating Addiction

Today there are various methods of treating the disease of addiction. The traditional method, the one I chose, is Alcoholics Anonymous. It is a program consisting of twelve steps and principles and a higher power—I chose God. You're higher power can be anything or anyone—God or the Universe or the sun or the sky.

I went to detox and then rehab; I was gone for a longer time than most, but I was sicker than most. After rehab I continued to attend meetings every day for six months. I loved being with a group of people who understood my struggle, people who struggled right along with me and supported me. I understood that I was powerless over alcohol and my life was unmanageable. There were other people who had done bad things in their lives and they taught me how to live and deal with the pain and the feelings of hopelessness—AA saved my life.

An alternative treatment to AA involves medications. The newest one is the Pennsylvania Model that embraces pharmacotherapy as a cornerstone of treatment along with individual and group psychological treatment and support. They compare the program to a three-legged stool. The three legs are the biological, psychological and social components of recovery. Each leg is just as important as the others. Take one leg away and the stool is defective.

The biological component involves the physical addiction to the drug of choice, for example the shakes you get when your body is telling you to take that drug. Anything that is mind altering is a drug—a drug is a drug is a drug. When a user stops using, he or she will experience both physical and psychological pain. The ACA says it's the emotional issues caused by the imbalances in the brain that cause relapse. This is a very dangerous component of the disease and very common. It leads right back to the same consequences. It is difficult for the social drinker to understand why alcohol-dependent people drink when they are aware of the consequences.

Medication deals with the biological aspect of the alcoholic. Naltrexone is a common drug being used; they call it the wonder drug because it has been known to control the cravings.

Psychotherapy addresses the emotional aspect and helps the addict handle the otherwise overwhelming avalanche of emotions. We stop growing emotionally when we start drinking and when we stop we are in the same place we started.

Another drug being used to treat addiction is called Antabuse, but rather than addressing the biological side of addiction, it makes the person violently ill when they consume alcohol.

Substance use disorders are complex problems; people with these disorders were once thought to have a character defect or moral weakness. Most scientists and researchers now consider alcohol and drug dependence to be a long-term illness. No matter how you slice it, seeking treatment is no treat. It's scary, it's painful, and it's lonely. But, it's necessary! It's the best way to truly enter recovery and maintain sobriety.